文化解读

趣说英语习语

杨 昆——著

中国书籍出版社
China Book Press

图书在版编目 (CIP) 数据

文化解读：趣说英语习语 / 杨昆著 . -- 北京：中国书籍出版社，2022.7

ISBN 978-7-5068-9064-9

Ⅰ . ①文⋯ Ⅱ . ①杨⋯ Ⅲ . ①英语 - 社会习惯语 - 通俗读物 Ⅳ . ① H313.3-49

中国版本图书馆 CIP 数据核字（2022）第 110582 号

文化解读：趣说英语习语

杨　昆 著

责任编辑	宋　然
责任印制	孙马飞　马　芝
封面设计	仙　境
出版发行	中国书籍出版社
地　　址	北京市丰台区三路居路 97 号 (邮编：100073)
电　　话	（010）52257143（总编室）　　（010）52257140（发行部）
电子邮箱	eo@chinabp.com.cn
经　　销	全国新华书店
印　　厂	三河市德贤弘印务有限公司
开　　本	710 毫米 × 1000 毫米　1/16
字　　数	157 千字
印　　张	14.25
版　　次	2023 年 3 月第 1 版
印　　次	2023 年 3 月第 1 次印刷
书　　号	ISBN 978-7-5068-9064-9
定　　价	56.00 元

版权所有　　翻印必究

前 言

很多学习英语的人总会有这样的困惑：明明学了多年英语，但在交流或写作时，语言总是显得很苍白，不够地道。你有没有这样的困惑呢？其实，这很有可能是因为没有掌握英语这门语言的精华——习语。

你知道什么是习语吗？学习英语为何要掌握英语习语呢？

其实，习语（idiom）就是那些长期被人们使用而沉淀形成的形式固定、语义深刻的短语或词组。习语是语言的精华，其简洁明快，生动形象，言简义丰，读来趣味无穷；习语更是文化的核心，其文化意蕴浓厚，民族色彩鲜明。认识和学习英语习语，能够积累更多实用的短语和词组，深入了解英语文化，进而让表达更加生动和地道。可见，了解、掌握和使用习语是非常有必要的。

对于迫切想要提升英语表达能力的你而言，本书将会提供很大帮助。本书汇聚了英语中的众多经典习语，包括源自神话传说、寓言故事、文学作品、风俗习惯、动植物等的各类习语，能够加深你对英语

习语的认识和了解。

  本书不仅注重知识的呈现，也注重知识的运用，"学以致用"版块能够让你在学习习语的同时学会加以使用，让你完全掌握习语知识。而"习语故事"版块更是使习语的趣味性与文化性得以充分展现，能够增强阅读乐趣，让你感知习语背后的文化意蕴。

  如果你也想让自己的英语表达更地道、更出色，那么就来阅读本书，相信你定能有所收获，英语综合水平会得到明显提升。

作者

2022 年 4 月

目 录

前言 / I

第一章　趣说与神话、寓言、宗教信仰有关的习语 / 001

文化背景解读 / 003

趣说古希腊罗马神话与习语 / 007

趣说寓言故事与习语 / 015

趣说宗教信仰与习语 / 021

知识活学活用 / 026

第二章　隐藏在文学作品与历史典故中的习语 / 031

文化背景解读 / 033

趣说文学作品与习语 / 036

趣说历史典故与习语 / 045

知识活学活用 / 054

第三章　随经济与科技发展而来的习语 / 059

文化背景解读 / 061

趣说经济与习语 / 063

趣说科技与习语 / 070

知识活学活用 / 080

第四章　孕育于自然环境和风俗习惯中的习语 / 083

文化背景解读 / 085

趣说自然环境与习语 / 088

趣说风俗习惯与习语 / 096

知识活学活用 / 106

第五章　根植于动物与植物的习语 / 111

文化背景解读 / 113

趣说动物与习语 / 115

趣说植物与习语 / 125

知识活学活用 / 134

第六章　妙趣横生的颜色与地名习语 / 137

文化背景解读 / 139

趣说颜色与习语 / 141

趣说地名与习语 / 150

知识活学活用 / 159

第七章　趣说与身体、职业相关的习语 / 163

文化背景解读 / 165

趣说身体与习语 / 167

趣说职业与习语 / 177

知识活学活用 / 186

第八章　读懂与体育、娱乐运动有关的习语 / 189

文化背景解读 / 191

趣说体育运动与习语 / 194

趣说娱乐运动与习语 / 203

知识活学活用 / 212

参考文献 / 216

第一章

趣说与神话、寓言、宗教信仰有关的习语

习语是语言中一种独特的存在，虽短小精练，但妙趣横生，而且有着深厚的历史文化渊源。

习语与古希腊罗马神话、寓言故事、宗教信仰等有着密切的联系。古希腊罗马神话丰富生动，寓言故事趣味十足，宗教信仰影响深远，习语从中而生，既丰富了英语语言，又映射了英语文化，极富民族特色。

文化背景解读

习语并不是凭空产生的，而是有一定文化渊源的，其中很多习语就源自古希腊罗马神话、寓言故事和宗教信仰，与它们渊源颇深。

缘起古希腊罗马神话

古希腊可谓西方文明的重要源头，西方的众多文学、艺术等都源自古希腊。其中，古希腊神话是最早的一种文学形式，讲述了关于古希腊的神、英雄、自然等传说和故事，丰富生动，易于传播。古希腊

神话最初一直以口头的形式被古希腊人传播着，之后通过各种著作记录下来，并逐渐趋于成熟。在古希腊神话中，众神有着同人一样的形态和思想情感，同时有着不朽的力量，人在他们的面前显得极其渺小。古希腊神话中有十二主神，他们的故事是古希腊神话的重要内容。

古罗马神话是基于古希腊神话而形成的，当古希腊人移居意大利之后，将文化艺术也带到了这里，古罗马人开始学习古希腊文化，并将古希腊神话的内容移植到古罗马神话中，形成了独具特色的古希腊罗马神话。一直以来，古希腊罗马神话在西方文化中是明珠般的存在，滋养着西方文化，推动着西方文化的发展，同时也深深地影响了西方语言。

很多的英语习语都源自古希腊罗马神话，这些习语生动形象，寓意深刻，不仅丰富了西方语言，也反映了西方的文化历史。

习语知识

古希腊神话中有十二主神，很多神话故事都是围绕他们展开的。古希腊神话中的十二主神具体包括：众神之王宙斯（Zeus），天后赫拉（Hera），智慧与战争女神雅典娜（Athena），海神波塞冬（Poseidon），光明、音乐、预言与医药之神阿波罗（Apollo），狩猎女神阿尔忒弥斯（Artemis），战争之神阿瑞斯（Ares），爱情和美丽女神阿佛洛狄

忒（Aphrodite），火焰和工匠之神赫菲斯托斯（Hephaestus），炉灶和家庭女神赫斯提亚（Hestia），商业、旅者和畜牧之神赫尔墨斯（Hermes），农业和丰收女神德墨忒尔（Demeter）。

习语与寓言故事的渊源

寓言是一种文学表现形式，通过将动物或事物拟人化来讲述某个道理。寓言故事既言简意赅，又蕴含着深刻的寓意，许多已成为广为流传的文学作品。

其中，最为著名的要数《伊索寓言》，伊索是公元前6世纪古希腊的一位寓言家，他经常为大家讲述各式各样的故事，这些故事大多以动物为主角，生动形象，其中所包含的哲理思想，常常给人们以警示，让人听后记忆深刻。伊索的寓言故事渐渐流传开来。后来，古希腊罗马的作家将这些寓言故事进行汇编，便形成了广为流传的《伊索寓言》。

寓言为英语习语的形成做出了巨大的贡献，很多习语都是寓言故事浓缩升华而成的，这类习语往往生动形象，寓意深远。

宗教信仰对习语的影响

宗教是一种社会意识形态。信奉宗教的人们常将自己对一切的希

望寄托于宗教信仰，将自己的感情系于自己所信奉的宗教，祈求消除苦恼不安，获得希望与安心。在西方的宗教文化中，基督教是最大的宗教之一。基督教的教义多是出自《圣经》，《圣经》也成为西方宗教文化中十分重要的经典。

　　宗教信仰是西方文化的重要组成部分，已经融入了人们的精神生活和社会生活，并对语言产生了重要影响。西方宗教信仰促使了许多习语的产生，并在语言文化发展中留下了深刻的印痕。

趣说古希腊罗马神话与习语

古希腊罗马神话给人类留下了珍贵的故事遗产,对西方文化和文明产生了深刻的影响,并为后来的人们认识古希腊和古罗马以及欧洲文化提供了一个窗口。

与此同时,丰富的古希腊罗马神话衍生了丰富的习语,从这些习语中可以深切地感受到古希腊罗马神话的精神文化。下面就一起来看看与古希腊罗马神话相关的习语的风采。

under the aegis of
在……庇护下；由……主办

学以致用

The school has established more than 30 clubs to enrich students' extracurricular life under the aegis of the principal.

在校长的支持下，学校成立了30多个社团来丰富学生的课余生活。

We knew the work plans might change once we started to work under the aegis of the new hotel manager.

我们都知道，一旦新的酒店经理接手我们的工作，原来的工作计划可能会发生变化。

When the earthquake occurred, the students were able to evacuate safely under the aegis of their teachers.

地震发生时，在老师的庇护下，学生得以安全撤离。

习语故事

"under the aegis of"源自古希腊神话，传说"aegis"是主神宙斯的神盾，这块神盾无坚不摧，法力无边。宙斯只要微微晃动神盾，天空

便会乌云密布，电闪雷鸣，狂风大作。敌人都闻风丧胆，纷纷畏惧宙斯的神盾。每次危险将至，神盾都可以发挥其庇护的作用。"under the aegis of"字面意思就是"在神盾之下"，具体表示"在……的庇佑下；在……的支持下"。

Midas touch
点石成金；赚大钱的本领

学以致用

Investors always want teachers who can teach them how to have the Midas touch.
投资者总是想要能够教给他们赚大钱的方法的老师。

The man is a young property developer with the Midas touch.
这个男人是一位房地产开发商，年纪轻轻就有赚大钱的本领。

Mark had the Midas touch. He started a business by setting up a stall in the open air and in a year he was a millionaire.
马克有赚大钱的本领，他从露天摆摊开始创业，一年后就成了百万富翁。

习语故事

"Midas touch"源自古希腊神话，传说小亚细亚中西部有一个古国叫作弗里吉亚，国王名叫迈达斯（Midas），他十分贪恋财宝，一心只想成为世界上最富有的人。

酒神狄俄尼索斯为报答迈达斯曾经帮助过他恩师的情义，便答应帮助他，赐予了迈达斯"点物成金"的本领，迈达斯所触摸到的一切都变成了金子，最后甚至连他的小女儿都变成了金子。

迈达斯十分懊悔，便求酒神解除他的法术。酒神最后便收回了他的法力，一切才恢复了原样。后来，人们便将"Midas touch"引申为"点石成金；赚大钱的本领"。

apple of discord
争端的起因；祸根

学以致用

In many poor families, the economy becomes the apple of discord between husband and wife.
在很多贫困的家庭中，夫妻不和的原因大多是经济问题。

Billy and John used to be good friends, but since the original general manager left, who will be the general manager has become the apple of discord.
比利和约翰原本是好朋友，但自从原来的总经理离职后，总经理的位置由谁来坐就成为他们纷争的起因。

The wealth of father becomes the apple of discord between the two brothers.
父亲的财产成了两兄弟不和的根源。

习语故事

"apple of discord"出自古希腊神话。传说海神之女西蒂斯和阿尔戈英雄珀琉斯举行婚礼时，没有邀请专司不和的女神厄里斯。厄里斯十分愤怒，决心报复他们，便在席间投下了一个金苹果，上面刻着"献

给最美丽的人"。

而来参加婚礼的有三位女神，分别是天后赫拉、智慧女神雅典娜以及爱与美的女神阿佛洛狄忒。这三位女神都认为自己才是最美丽的人，几番争执不下，就请来特洛伊王子帕里斯进行评判。帕里斯把金苹果判给了阿佛洛狄忒，于是天后和智慧女神十分愤怒，发誓要向特洛伊发动战争。

因为一个金苹果，特洛伊与古希腊开始了历时十年的战争。后来人们便用"apple of discord"来指代"争端的起因；祸根"。

cut the Gordian knot
快刀斩乱麻

学以致用

William often thinks of simple solutions when the rest of us are struggling with details. He has a talent for cutting the Gordian knot.

当我们其他人都在为细节而纠结时，威廉经常能想到简单的解决方案。他很擅长快刀斩乱麻。

Since things are imminent, the problem can only be solved by cutting the Gordian knot.

事情既已迫在眉睫，唯有快刀斩乱麻，才能解决问题。

After she cut the Gordian knot and dealt with these disturbing problems, she felt extremely relieved.

她快刀斩乱麻地处理掉这些困扰人的问题后，内心感到无比轻松。

习语故事

"cut the Gordian knot"出自古希腊神话。传说小亚细亚弗里吉亚的国王戈尔迪（Gordian）在神庙外的树上绑了个绳结，这个绳结十分巧妙，很难找到绳头解开。神预言，谁能解开绳结，就可统治亚洲。众人前仆后继，尝试解开 the Gordian knot，均未成功。

直到后来，公元前4世纪，马其顿国王远征东方时，路过神庙。人们告诉他神的预言，他随手拔出了佩剑，将这绳结砍了开来，人们都十分震惊。

根据这一传说，后人用"the Gordian knot"比作"难以解决的问题"，而"cut the Gordian knot"就是指"用大刀阔斧的办法解决问题"。这一习语与汉语中的"快刀斩乱麻"有异曲同工之妙。

习语知识

古希腊罗马神话故事是西方文化中最为独特的部分，除了上述习语外，还有部分习语也源自古希腊罗马神话，我们一起来看一下吧。

halcyon days　美好时光

这一习语源自古希腊神话，风神埃俄罗斯之女海尔塞妮（Halcyon）和她的丈夫刻宇克斯恩爱非常。但有一次，丈夫刻宇克斯出海后一直未归。海尔塞妮十分担忧，在某天夜里，睡梦之神摩尔甫斯托梦给她，告诉她刻宇克斯已经不幸遭遇海难。她悲痛欲绝，纵身跳入了大海之中。天神为其痴情所感动，便将她与丈夫都变成了翠鸟，在海上建立了新的家庭。以后，每当翠鸟在海上筑巢产卵，也就是每年冬至前七天和后七天的时间里，海上总是风平浪静。人们将这段"平安时期"称为"halcyon days"。后来，"halcyon days"也用来比喻"太平岁月；美好时光"。

labor of Sisyphus　永无休止的苦工

这一习语源自古希腊神话，传说西西弗斯（Sisyphus）是古希腊奴隶制城邦柯林斯的一个暴君。他生前剥削百姓，死后被罚推巨石上山，但每次巨石都会在临近山顶的时候滚落下来。因此，他只能重新再推，如此反复循环，永无休止。

趣说寓言故事与习语

　　寓言故事形式简练，寓意深远，流传甚广。通过将这些寓言故事浓缩升华，形成了许多相关的习语。

　　这些习语生动形象，引人入胜，而且蕴含着深刻的道理，给人以启发。了解和掌握这些习语，将能有效提升英语水平。下面就让我们一起来学习一下吧。

文化解读：趣说英语习语

fish in troubled waters
浑水摸鱼；趁火打劫

学以致用

Those who are greedy for profit always want to fish in troubled waters and gain benefits from it.

那些利欲熏心的人总是想着浑水摸鱼，从中获利。

The station was crowded with people, and when there were so many people, the thief was fishing in troubled waters and tried to steal the tourists' mobile phones.

车站人来人往，趁着人多，小偷浑水摸鱼想要偷走游客的手机。

Recently, many objective factors have caused our company to fall into crisis, and rival companies are likely to be fishing in troubled waters at this time. We must be vigilant.

最近，很多客观因素导致我们公司陷入危机，对手公司很可能会在此时趁火打劫，我们一定要警惕。

习语故事

"fish in troubled waters"出自《伊索寓言·渔夫》，讲的是有个渔夫在河里张网捕鱼，他把网支在河道中央，然后用一根绳子拴上石头，扔到河里搅动，导致河水中的泥沙泛起，河水中的鱼儿都惊慌逃窜，慌忙之中落进渔网。渔夫用这个方法捕获了很多鱼，但是也导致河水变得浑浊不堪。

附近的居民怨声载道，问他"你把河水都搅浑了，让我们去哪里找清水饮用呢？"他却不以为意。后来，人们常用"fish in troubled waters"来比喻"试图从混乱状态中为自己赢得利益；利用别人的不幸达到自己的目的"。

add insult to injury
雪上加霜

学以致用

He had just experienced a divorce storm recently, and his mother had a car accident, which adds insult to injury.

他最近刚刚经历了离婚风波，母亲又出了车祸，真是雪上加霜，苦不

堪言。

Mary was recently unemployed and at home, but her daughter was diagnosed with a serious illness at this time, requiring huge medical bills, and the family's economy can be said to add insult to injury.

玛丽最近失业在家，但她的女儿刚好此时被诊断出患了重病，需要巨额的医疗费用，这个家庭的经济可以说是雪上加霜。

Even if you encounter difficulties, you must face them positively. A negative attitude will only add insult to injury.

就算遇到了困难，也要积极地面对，消极的态度只会让你雪上加霜。

习语故事

"add insult to injury"源自古罗马寓言中苍蝇和秃子的故事，讲的是有一个秃子的头上落下了一只苍蝇，这个秃子便去打苍蝇，但是苍蝇闪躲得飞快，秃子不仅没打着，还打伤了自己的头。于是人们便用"add insult to injury"这一习语来比喻有人本就遭遇不幸，却还有灾难降临。

look before one's leap
三思而后行；深思熟虑

学以致用

The questions raised by the teachers in class are a bit complicated, and the students need to look carefully before their leap after class.
老师在课堂上提出来的问题有些复杂，学生需要在课后深思熟虑。

If you want to be successful, you have to look before your leap.
如果你想要成功，那么你就必须要三思而后行。

When choosing a major to study at university, you must look before your leap.
在选择大学所要学习的专业时，一定要深思熟虑后再做决定。

习语故事

"look before one's leap"源自寓言故事《狐狸和山羊》。在故事中，一只狐狸被困在井里，于是便设法诱使一只山羊也跳下去。一旦山羊进了井里，狐狸就会爬到它的背上逃出井，让山羊陷入困境。因此，山羊在跳下去之前，就必须经过深思熟虑。"look before one's leap"多用来表达一种警告，即一个人不应该轻率行事，应首先考虑所有可能的后果。

文化解读：趣说英语习语

习语知识

源自寓言故事的习语还有很多，除了上述习语，还有部分习语也十分生动形象，让我们一起来看一下吧。

sour grapes　自欺欺人

这一习语源自寓言故事《狐狸与葡萄》。在一个炎热的夏日，狐狸经过一个果园，停在了葡萄架前，它想要吃葡萄，于是后退了几步，向前一冲，跳起来，却没有摘到葡萄。狐狸试了又试，都没有成功。于是它就开始安慰自己，说"这些葡萄肯定是酸的"。后来，人们就用"sour grapes"来讽刺那些得不到某些事物就说这些事物不好的人。

the snake and the eagle　善有善报

这一习语源自寓言故事《蛇与老鹰》。一条蛇和一只老鹰在拼死搏斗，老鹰被蛇紧紧勒住，眼看着就要死了，紧要关头一位农夫救了老鹰。从此，蛇对农夫心怀怨恨，于是就将毒液喷到农夫喝水的杯子里，想要毒害农夫。就在农夫要喝水时，老鹰飞了过来将农夫手中的杯子抓走了。之后，人们就用"the snake and the eagle"这一习语表示"善有善报"。

趣说宗教信仰与习语

宗教信仰是西方文化中十分重要的部分，体现了西方的文化特色。源自宗教信仰的习语十分常见，这些习语内涵极其丰富，折射出宗教对语言的影响，也反映了西方文化的独特之处。了解与宗教信仰有关的习语不仅有助于加深对西方文化的认识，也有助于英语水平的提升。下面就让我们一起来学习一下吧。

in seventh heaven
十分高兴；非常幸福

学以致用

A little child with a chocolate will think that he is in seventh heaven.

给小孩子一块巧克力，他就会觉得很开心。

Mira was in seventh heaven when she won the lottery!

米拉中了彩票，她真是高兴极了！

The reduction of pressure points and the relaxation of your joints will send you to seventh heaven.

释放压力，松弛关节，你会感到无比轻松。

习语故事

"in seventh heaven"是与宗教信仰有关的习语。西方人认为，天有七重，越往上越幸福。因此，后来人们便以"seventh heaven"（七重天）来比喻"极乐之地"，"in seventh heaven"也就喻指"十分开心；非常幸福"。

baptism of fire
严峻的考验

学以致用

This exam was the last mock exam before the college entrance examination, and it was baptism of fire for me.

这次的考试是高考前的最后一次模拟考试，对我来说是一次严峻的考验。

If Mark wants to become an excellent biological expert, he must participate in this field trip, which is baptism of fire for him, and only after this test can he improve.

马克要想成为优秀的生物专家，就必须参加这次野外考察，这对他来说是一次严峻的考验，只有经历了这次考验他才能进步。

Heavy rains have been falling for several days in a row, which is very unfavorable for search and rescue work and baptism of fire for rescuers.

连续几天暴雨下个不停，这对于搜救工作十分不利，对救援人员来说是严峻的考验。

习语故事

"baptism of fire"是与基督教有关的习语,其中"baptism"是"洗礼"的意思。在《马太福音》中,"baptism of fire"最早表示使有罪之人悔改。后来,巴里·爱德华·奥米拉博士在撰写有关拿破仑的回忆录时用"baptism of fire"(火的洗礼)来形容士兵遇到的艰难的考验,自此这一习语开始表示"严峻的考验"。

习语知识

除了上述习语,还有部分习语也与宗教信仰相关,下面一起来学习一下吧。

in the lap of the gods　听天由命

这是与基督教的天神有关的习语,其中"in the lap of"表示的是"在……的掌握之中",因此"in the lap of the gods"的字面意思也就是"在天神的掌握之中"。天神在西方宗教文化中被认为是造物主,是一切的主宰者,神之力是人力不可企及的。因此,"in the lap of the gods"也就表示一切在天神的掌握之中,人无能为力,喻指"听天由命"。

in one's Sunday best　　穿上盛装

　　这是与西方宗教文化中的礼拜相关的习语,礼拜是基督教重要的宗教活动,而每个礼拜天(Sunday)人们都要穿上自己最好的衣服参与。因此,后来人们就用"Sunday best"来比喻盛装、华服。

知识活学活用

在学习了与古希腊罗马神话、寓言故事和宗教信仰相关的习语后,下面来具体运用一下吧。

1. 将下列句子译成中文。

(1) For couples with children, the child's education can often be an apple of discord.

(2) We met by chance at the party that day, and all of a sudden I was reminded of those halcyon days we had between us.

(3) The thief dressed up as a student and entered the student dormitory to fish in troubled waters and steal.

（4）Not only has Mark recently lost his job, but he has also been seriously ill, which adds insult to injury.

（5）During Chinese New Year, the children are in seventh heaven.

（6）I have tried my best to prepare for this exam, as for the final result, it is in the lap of the gods.

（7）Mary really has the Midas touch, and every investment of hers is very successful.

（8）Although he knew that the cost of this plan would be very high, after looking before their leap, he chose the current plan.

2. 将下列句子译成英文。

（1）在出现紧急情况时，我们应该快刀斩乱麻，尽快做出决断，争分夺秒。

（2）年少的我们一起在学校度过了很多美好的时光。

（3）总有一些商贩趁着自然灾害发生的时候哄抬物价，这种行为十分不道德。

（4）年轻人应该经过深思熟虑以后再结婚，这是对夫妻双方负责。

（5）老板经过这次严峻的考验，发现他的确可以担负重任，他真的具有坚强的意志和惊人的毅力。

（6）明日便是毕业舞会了，同学们都挑选了自己最好看的衣服，准备盛装出席。

（7）如果我们只是把希望寄托在别人身上，那可能就是听天由命了。

参考译文

1. 译文如下。

（1）对于有了孩子的夫妻而言，孩子的教育问题往往可能会成为他们吵架的原因。

（2）那天的聚会上我们偶然相遇，突然间我想起了我们之间的那些美好时光。

（3）这个小偷打扮成学生的样子进入学生宿舍浑水摸鱼，进行盗窃。

（4）马克最近不但失业，又生了重病，可真是雪上加霜。

（5）对于孩子们来说，过年是一件开心的事。

（6）我已经竭尽全力地在准备这次考试了，至于最终的结果就听天由命吧。

（7）玛丽果然很有赚大钱的本事，她的每一项投资都很成功。

（8）尽管他知道这个方案的成本会十分高昂，但是经过深思熟虑后，他还是选择了现在的方案。

2. 译文如下。

（1）In the event of an emergency, we should cut the Gordian knot, make a decision as soon as possible, and race against time.

（2）We had halcyon days together at school when we were young.

（3）There are always some vendors who take advantage of natural disasters and fish in troubled waters to drive up prices, which is very unethical.

（4）Before getting married, young people should look before their leap, which is responsible for both husband and wife.

（5）After this baptism of fire, the boss found that he can indeed take on heavy responsibilities. He really has a strong will and amazing perseverance.

（6）Tomorrow is the prom, and the students have chosen their best clothes and are ready to get dressed up in their Sunday best.

（7）If we just pin our hopes on others, it may be in the lap of the gods.

第二章 CHAPTER 2

隐藏在文学作品与历史典故中的习语

文学作品和历史典故都是传达文化的方式，是民族文化重要的组成部分，它们丰富了人们的精神生活，陶冶了人们的情操，还衍生了大量的习语，丰富了语言并推动了语言的发展。这些习语往往发人深省，给人带来启示。

文化背景解读

源自文学作品与历史典故的英语习语非常多,这些习语凝结了西方文化的精华,也极大地丰富了英语语言文化。

文学作品与习语

文学作品对习语的形成有很大的影响,源自文学作品的习语也非常多。大致来讲,来自文学作品中的习语主要分为两种。一种是文学大家所作的著作中的经典语言,这些著作中有很多脍炙人口的语句,

这些语句逐渐形成了习语。例如，很多的英语习语源自英国作家莎士比亚的巨作，这也是因为他的作品语言丰富，生动优美，极富表现力。

第二种是有些文学作品的故事情节给人们留下了深刻的印象，经过传颂，慢慢变成了人们口中的习语；或者是文学作品中的经典角色，这些角色个性鲜明，甚至提到这些角色就能联想到其象征意义。例如，"man Friday"指的是忠实的仆人，这个习语来自笛福的著作《鲁滨逊漂流记》中忠实奴仆的名字。

习语知识

威廉·莎士比亚是文艺复兴时期英国著名的剧作家、诗人，他的作品部部经典，堪称举世之作。莎士比亚早期作品以喜剧和历史剧为主，其喜剧代表作有《仲夏夜之梦》《威尼斯商人》《无事生非》等，中后期主要以悲剧为主，其四大悲剧代表作《奥赛罗》《哈姆雷特》《李尔王》《麦克白》被认为是英语文学的经典之作。莎士比亚的文学作品揭示了人的本质，也展示了人性的缺陷，对后世文学发展产生了深刻的影响。

历史典故与习语

历史典故指的是关于历史事件、历史人物等的故事，具有浓厚的文化色彩。西方文化中的历史典故多是来自《圣经》、古希腊的传说和历史事件等。

历史典故浓缩了西方社会的历史，并衍生出众多脍炙人口的习语，这些与历史典故相关的习语也很好地体现了西方文化的特色。英语中与历史典故相关的习语是英语学习中丰富的宝藏，它们精辟，生动，形象，无论在书面表达还是口语表达中，都发挥着重要的作用。

趣说文学作品与习语

文学作品中的故事生动，语言优美，很多来自文学作品的英语习语都十分生动形象。下面我们一起来学习一下这些源于文学作品的习语吧。

wear one's heart on one's sleeve
感情流露；直抒胸臆

学以致用

He dares to wear his heart on his sleeve and that's what we admire about him.
他敢于直抒胸臆，这就是我们钦佩他的地方。

I know he wears his heart on his sleeve and I know he's a good manager.
我知道他心直口快，他是位好领导。

My sister's never been too shy to wear her heart on her sleeve but I'm the opposite.
我姐姐从来不会羞于表达自己的情感，而我恰恰相反。

习语故事

"wear one's heart on one's sleeve"这一习语出自莎士比亚的剧作《奥赛罗》，其字面意思是"将心意穿在袖子上"，实际意思是把自己的感情公开，不隐藏自己的情感。这一习语最早与比武有关，古代骑士在比武时会携带爱人赠送的信物，有时会在手臂上绑上手帕。最早使用这一说法的就是莎士比亚，由于《奥赛罗》被广泛流传，因此这一习语也流传至今。

live off the fat of the land
养尊处优

学以致用

If I had a million dollars, I'd invest it and live off the fat of the land.
如果我有一百万美元，我就会做投资，过上养尊处优的生活。

He won the lottery and began to live off the fat of the land.

他中了彩票，开始过起了养尊处优的生活。

The original intention of this show is to change the bad habits of these children who live off the fat of the land in daily life.

这档节目的初衷就是为了改变这些平日里过着锦衣玉食生活的孩子们的不良习惯。

习语故事

"live off the fat of the land" 这一习语源自《圣经》中的开篇之作《创世记》。而这一习语的流传始于约翰·斯坦贝克的中篇小说《人鼠之间》，小说中乔治对莱尼说："We'll live off the fat of the land and have rabbits when we make enough money to stop travelling around for work." "live off the fat of the land" 指的是靠肥沃的土地就能过上富足的好日子，因此后来人们便用这一习语来表示"养尊处优"。

green-eyed monster
嫉妒

学以致用

The green-eyed monster made her suffer when she learnt that you had moved into an upscale community.

听说你搬进了高档社区,她嫉妒得不得了。

The green-eyed monster can destroy a perfect relationship, and true friends appreciate each other.

嫉妒会破坏一段完美的关系,真正的朋友是相互欣赏的。

Carl has really been bitten by the green-eyed monster. He gets jealous if his wife so much as talks to another man.

卡尔真的很容易吃醋,甚至如果他的妻子和另一个男人说话,他都会嫉妒。

习语故事

"green-eyed monster"源自莎士比亚的戏剧《威尼斯商人》,女主人公鲍西娅在对自己的爱人巴萨尼奥的一段独白中便提及了"green-eyed monster",用"green-eyed monster"来比喻猜疑嫉妒之心。而后来,莎士比亚在悲剧《奥赛罗》中,再一次使用了"green-eyed monster"来比喻反派伊阿古的妒忌心。

applaud/cheer someone to the echo
掌声雷动；大声喝彩

学以致用

Her dance performance was wonderful, and the audience applauded her to the echo.
她的舞蹈表演十分精彩，台下掌声雷动。

She was very happy that Jack finally returned to the game after recovering from injury, and the fans in the audience were applauding him to the echo.
她很高兴看到杰克在伤愈后终于又重返了赛场，台下的粉丝都在为他加油助威。

He was in control in the first half and his followers cheered him to the echo.
他在上半场比赛时就控制住了局面，他的支持者都在为他喝彩。

习语故事

"applaud someone to the echo"是来自莎士比亚剧作《麦克白》中的一句台词："I would applaud thee to the very echo that should applaud again."后来这一习语就有了"大声喝彩,掌声雷动"的意思。这一习语中的"applaud"也可以用"cheer"来代替。

all hell breaks loose
失控

学以致用

When the fire spread to the pigsty, the pigs in the pigsty all fled, and all hell broke loose.

当大火蔓延到猪圈时,猪圈里的猪都四散逃开,场面一度失控。

I happened to pass by that pub on Saturday night and all hell broke loose outside the pub.

周六晚上,我碰巧路过那家酒吧,看到那家酒吧外面一片混乱。

This big guy walked up to the bar and hit Freddie, and suddenly all hell broke loose.

这个大块头走到吧台前,打了弗雷迪,突然间,场面一片混乱。

习语故事

"all hell breaks loose"源自著名诗人约翰·弥尔顿的诗作《失乐园》。"all hell breaks loose"的字面意思是"地狱疏于管理",这是一种夸张的表达,表示状况已经超出了极限,不受控制了。"all hell"在这里指的是问题和混乱情况,而"breaks loose"则表示事情已经不受控制,无法管理。

pot calling the kettle black
半斤八两;五十步笑百步

学以致用

I can't believe that you are upset because I was late and we arrived at the company at the same time. That is the pot calling the kettle black.

我不敢相信你居然因为我迟到而生气,我们差不多时间到的公司,这简直是五十步笑百步。

I agree that it's rude. However, this is like the pot calling the kettle black because I sometimes do the same thing to you.

我觉得这是不礼貌的。但是,我有时也会对你做同样的事情,咱俩半斤八两。

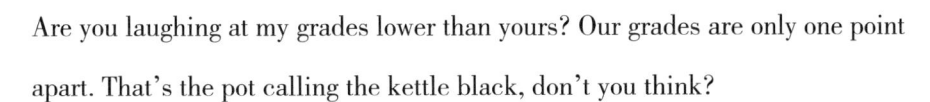

Are you laughing at my grades lower than yours? Our grades are only one point apart. That's the pot calling the kettle black, don't you think?

你在嘲笑我考的成绩比你低？咱俩的成绩就差一分，你不觉得这是五十步笑百步吗？

习语故事

"pot calling the kettle black"这一习语最早源自塞万提斯的小说《堂吉诃德》，后来莎士比亚的戏剧《特洛伊罗斯与克瑞西达》中也使用了这一习语。"pot calling the kettle black"的字面意思是"锅说壶是黑的"，在中世纪时期，厨房中的壶和锅都是由铁铸成的，它们在遇到火之后都会变黑，因此锅和壶都一样是黑黢黢的。这一习语讽刺的是那些只看到别人有错，而没有意识到自己的错误的人。

习语知识

除了上述习语，还有一些习语同样出自著名的文学作品，随着这些文学作品的传世，这些习语也流传至今。

a nine days' wonder　轰动一时即被遗忘的人或物

这一习语最早与古罗马的一个习俗有关，每当自然界出现异常现象的时候，罗马人就会认为这是不祥之兆。为了驱灾避祸，教会就会进行一场历时九天的祈祷仪式。这种祈祷仪式一般都会声势浩大，但是仪式过后人们恢复正常生活就会把这个事情忘掉。而这一习语之所以会广为流传，主要是因为莎士比亚在剧作中曾经诙谐地使用了这一习语，使得人们记忆深刻。

an albatross around one's neck　令人忧虑的事

这一习语源自18世纪的诗人柯勒律治的长诗《老水手之歌》，诗中说道信天翁（albatross）是非洲南部好望角一带的一种吉祥之鸟，但是一个水手失手误杀了一只信天翁，这是不吉利的，因此人们为了惩罚他，强制地将死去的信天翁挂在他的脖子上。后来，人们用"an albatross around one's neck"来表示无法摆脱的苦恼、令人忧虑的事情。

趣说历史典故与习语

历史上的很多典故都令人印象深刻,由此而来的习语也十分具有教育意义。下面就让我们一起来学习一下吧。

turn a blind eye
视而不见

学以致用

We cannot continue to turn a blind eye or ear and pretend that all is well when many people are being hurt and yearning for help.

当许多人受伤并渴望得到帮助时,我们不能继续视而不见或充耳不闻,假装一切没有发生。

Seeing a group of thugs beating an old man, he did not choose to turn a blind eye, but bravely chased away the thugs and sent the old man to the hospital in time.

看到一帮暴徒正在殴打一位老人,他没有选择视而不见,而是勇敢地赶走了暴徒,并且及时送老人去了医院。

If a girl turns a blind eye to your courtship, it probably means she doesn't like you.

如果一个女孩对你的示好视而不见,可能意味着她并不喜欢你。

习语故事

"turn a blind eye"典出历史事件,与英国海军霍雷肖·纳尔逊从军生涯中一场传奇的战役有关。1801年,在哥本哈根战役期间,纳尔逊被指派去抵抗丹麦的一支舰队。当时纳尔逊的长官向他挥动旗子示意他撤退,他却故意用看不见的那只眼睛对着望远镜,毫不在意长官的示意,继续战斗,最终取得了战役的胜利。后来,人们就用"turn a blind eye"表示故意对某事视而不见。

meet one's Waterloo
遭遇沉重打击

学以致用

They did their best to prepare for this match, but in the end they met their Waterloo.

为了这场比赛他们尽了最大的努力,但最终还是遭遇了惨败。

Caocao met his Waterloo in the Battle of Red Cliffs, and was chased by Liu Bei's subordinates, so he could only escape.

赤壁之战曹操遭遇惨败,被刘备的部下追赶,只能落荒而逃。

Due to the excellent films that aired during the New Year, the cartoon met its Waterloo.

由于新年期间播出的电影都很优秀,这部动画片的票房遭遇惨败。

习语故事

"meet one's Waterloo"典出著名历史战役——滑铁卢(Waterloo)战役,这场战役导致拿破仑惨败,从此一蹶不振。滑铁卢战役中反法联

军获得了胜利，改变了欧洲历史，结束了拿破仑帝国时代。因此，后来人们将"meet one's Waterloo"（遭遇滑铁卢）比喻遭遇惨烈的失败。

hang by a thread
岌岌可危；千钧一发

学以致用

Because I contradicted my boss on impulse to speak for my colleague, my job is hanging by a thread.

因为我为了帮同事说话一时冲动顶撞了上司，所以我的工作现在岌岌可危。

The life of the cancer patient is hanging by a thread despite all efforts of the doctors.

尽管医生们竭尽全力，这位癌症病人的生命仍岌岌可危。

After his drunken antics at the wedding, Fred's reputation was left hanging by a thread.

自从弗雷德醉酒在婚礼上胡闹之后，他的名誉岌岌可危。

习语故事

"hang by a thread"典出古希腊传说。公元前4世纪，西西里岛上的希腊城邦国家叙拉古有一名大臣名叫达摩克利斯，他非常羡慕君王的气派，常常幻想自己成为国王。

有一天，国王请他赴宴，并让他坐在了王座上。他一开始受宠若惊，欣喜若狂。但后来他抬头看见头顶上方用一根细线系着一把宝剑，随时都可能掉下来。顿时，他吓得魂飞魄散。国王做此安排是为了让他明白，即使身为君王，却仍然惶惶不可终日，随时有杀身之祸来临。

后来古罗马哲学家西塞罗在《图斯库鲁姆谈话录》中转述了这一传说，并将"hang by a thread"这一习语传播开来。后来，人们便用"hang by a thread"表示"岌岌可危"或"千钧一发"。

heap coals of fire on one's head
以德报怨；化干戈为玉帛

学以致用

This morning Anna got very mad at one of the girls but grandmother told her she ought to heap coals of fire on her head.

今天早上安娜跟一个女孩吵架了，但是祖母告诉她应该化干戈为玉帛。

Although he is young, he is very admirable for his ability to heap coals of fire on other's head regardless of his past suspicions.

他年纪虽轻，却能不计前嫌地以德报怨，令人十分钦佩。

Even if others have misunderstandings with us, we can't think of revenge on others all day long. If we learn to heap coals of fire on others' head, we will be respected by more people.

即使别人与我们有误会，我们也不能成天想着去报复别人。如果我们学会了以德报怨，将会得到更多人的尊重。

习语故事

"heap coals of fire on one's head"典出《圣经·箴言》第二十五章。

《圣经》中提倡人们以德报怨，用自己的善良来感化他人，融化怨恨的坚冰。因此，"heap coals of fire on one's head"后来被引申为"以德报怨；化干戈为玉帛"。

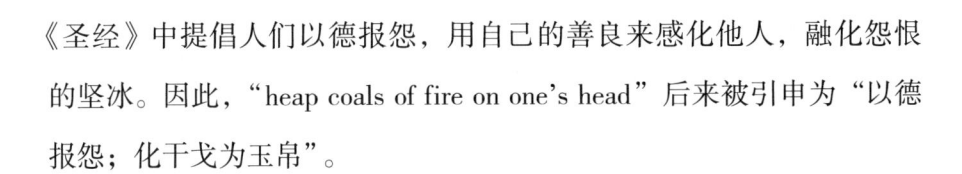

the apple of one's eye 掌上明珠

学以致用

John loved his little daughter very much, always regarded her as the apple of his eye, and never let her suffer any grievances.
约翰特别疼爱自己的小女儿，一直视她为掌上明珠，从来不让她受任何委屈。

He has always regarded these antiques as the apple of his eye, and you must tell the children not to play here, so as not to damage these antiques.
他一直把这些古董视为掌上明珠，你们一定要叮嘱孩子们不要在这里玩耍，以免碰坏了这些古董。

Many only children are regarded by their parents as the apple of their eyes, and they have always loved them, but they only pay attention to material satisfaction, which will encourage their children to be selfish and extravagant.
很多独生子女都被父母视为掌上明珠，父母对他们一直宠爱有加，但

是只重视物质方面的满足，会助长子女的自私和奢侈。

习语故事

"the apple of one's eye"典出《圣经》。古时候，人们认为眼睛中的瞳孔是一个"实心的球体"，人们常用"apple"（苹果）来表示眼睛的瞳孔。后来，人们开始广泛使用"the apple of one's eye"来比喻"珍贵的东西/人"，也就是"掌上明珠"的意思。

习语知识

除了上述这些出自典故的习语，还有一些习语同样经典，让我们一起看一下吧。

the writing on the wall　　不祥之兆

这一习语典出《旧约·但以理书》。《旧约》中记载，新巴比伦王国摄政王伯沙撒在宴饮时，忽然看到有一个神秘的手指在墙上书写着什么，国王看不懂，便叫来了预言家但以理。但以理看后大惊，墙上写的竟是"大难临头"。果真如预言所说，当晚国王便遭遇不幸。源于这一典故，后来人们便用"the writing on the wall"来表示"不祥之兆"。

a brand from the burning　　劫后余生

这一习语典出《阿摩司书》。阿摩司是公元前8世纪的先知，他曾严厉谴责以色列人的腐败，预言以色列王国的覆灭。他向以色列人

发出警告，劝他们不要一直犯错，应悔过自新。阿摩司说，如果他们一直不知悔改，他们的城池就会被颠覆，如同从前所多玛和阿摩拉的倾覆一样。以色列人十分感念这次警示，他们感觉自己好像"从火中抽出的一根柴"（a brand from the burning），幸免于被降灾。

知识活学活用

学习了这么多来自文学作品和历史典故的习语,让我们一起来运用一下吧。

1. 将下列句子译成中文。

(1) My favorite among these children is John. He wears his heart on his sleeve and always dares to express his emotions directly.

(2) He was used to live off the fat of the land since he was a child, and he never did anything by himself.

(3) His eloquent performance moved the audience, depicting the magical scenery of Yunnan, and the audience applauded him to the echo.

（4）Many actors only pay attention to their appearance and not their own abilities. If this continues for a long time, they will only become a nine days' wonder on the stage.

（5）His failing business has become an albatross around his neck.

（6）The company appears to be safe and sound, but that is not the case, mainly because the company's financial situation is hanging by a thread.

（7）Since Sarah took the initiative to heap coals of fire on Belle's head, the atmosphere in the office has become much more harmonious.

（8）After a brand from the burning, he loved life even more.

（9）He said that children are the apple of their parents' eyes, the miracle of life and the hope for the future.

2. 将下列句子译成英文。

（1）自从她丈夫掌管了公司以后，她就向单位提出了辞职，在家里过上了养尊处优的生活。

（2）她姐姐买了新车，她嫉妒得不得了。

（3）灯光亮起的一瞬间，舞台下热爱旗袍文化的观众的欢呼声不断，掌声雷动。

（4）台风过后，马路上多处信号灯出现了故障，道路状况一片混乱。

（5）尽管地铁站有明文规定不允许在车厢里吃东西，但有些人还是会视而不见。

（6）尽管女儿是琳达的掌上明珠，但是她依然对女儿严格要求。

（7）我整天无所事事，而哥哥整天游手好闲，我们俩真是半斤八两。

参考译文

1. 译文如下。

（1）这几个孩子里面我最喜欢的就是约翰，他心直口快，总是敢于直接表达自己的情感。

（2）他从小过惯了养尊处优的生活，凡事从不自己动手。

（3）他如歌如诉的演奏打动了观众，描绘了神奇的云南风光，现场掌声雷动。

（4）很多演员只注重外在而不注重自身的能力，如果长期这样下去他们只会成为舞台上昙花一现的人。

（5）生意失败成了他挥之不去的阴影。

（6）公司表面看起来安然无恙，但实际情况并非如此，这主要是因为公司财政状况已经岌岌可危了。

（7）自从莎拉主动与贝丽化干戈为玉帛后，办公室的气氛都和谐了很多。

（8）经过这次劫后余生，他更加热爱生命了。

（9）他说，孩子是父母的掌上明珠，是生命的奇迹，是未来的希望。

2. 译文如下。

（1）Since her husband took charge of the company, she has resigned from the company and has lived off the fat of the land.

（2）Her sister bought a new car and she was bitten by the green-eyed monster.

（3）The moment the lights came on, the audience who loved the cheongsam culture under the stage cheered and applauded them to the echo.

（4）After the typhoon, many signal lights on the road failed, and all hell broke loose on the road.

（5）Although the subway station has a clear rule that food is not allowed in the carriage, some people still turn a blind eye.

（6）Although Linda's daughter is the apple of her eye, she still has strict requirements for her daughter.

（7）I have nothing to do all day, and my brother is idle all day. That is the pot calling the kettle black.

第三章 CHAPTER 3

随经济与科技发展而来的习语

在社会前进的道路上，经济与科技在飞速地发展。为了适应快速发展的经济与科技，人们创造和组织了很多与之相关的语言，有些甚至成了脍炙人口的习语。这些习语蕴含着特定的含义，也反映着时代的变化。

文化背景解读

随经济与科技发展而来的习语，体现了经济和科技发展对人们生活模式的影响，同时透射出了人们的生活模式。

经济发展与习语

经济发展使得社会发生了极大的改变，也使得人们的生活模式发生了变化。随经济发展而来的英语习语中，很多都与美国的经济发展史密切相关。

很多习语是在美国西部开发的过程中诞生的，这些习语有些甚至

能够体现出美国经济发展的历程。例如"fly off the handle"这一习语便是在美国西部拓荒时期出现的,当时人们为了开垦土地,大量砍伐树木,因此当时很多家庭的常用工具都是斧头。其中"handle"便是指的斧头柄,斧头柄有时会因为力气过大而松脱飞落,后来便被人们用来表示失控而大发脾气的状况。

英美的经济发展也丰富了人们的语言文化,即使在今天人们所使用的习语中,依然能发现许多经济开发的痕迹。

科技发展与习语

科学技术的发展对人们的生活产生了极大的影响,科技发明推动了人类文明的发展。科技发明也推动着生产方式的变革,远古时期铁器的发明替代了石器,改变了人们的劳动方式;电力的发明极大地促进了社会的进步和发展,大大地改善了人们的生活质量;航空技术的发明优化了交通,便捷了生活;广播技术的发展使得信息传播更为迅速,便于人们快速获取信息。

科技发展与人们生活关系密切,也逐渐衍生了大量的习语。也正因为如此,习语才可以与时俱进。随着科技发展而产生的习语,也影响和丰富了语言文化。

趣说经济与习语

与经济相关的习语很多都是源于经济发展历程中所发生的事件,也有些习语是从金融经济等领域的专业术语中发展而来。

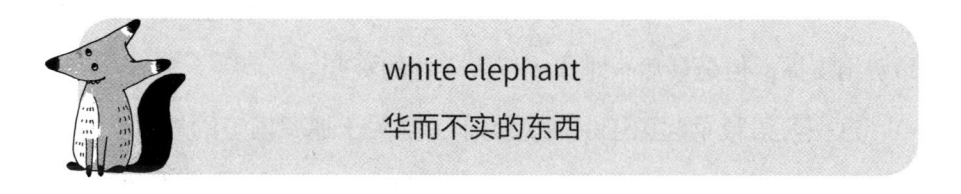

> white elephant
> 华而不实的东西

学以致用

Mark didn't want what he designed to be white elephants, so he wrote a questionnaire to find out what people wanted.

马克不想他设计的东西成为华而不实的东西，因此他特意编写了调查问卷，调查大家需要什么。

I found his new cabinets to be white elephants, with very little drawer space to hold anything at all.

我发现他新买的柜子简直华而不实，抽屉的空间很小，根本放不了什么东西。

Because the cost of the project was too high, but the benefits were too low, the boss thought the project might be nothing but a white elephant.

由于这个项目的成本过高，但收益又太低，因此老板认为这个项目可能华而不实。

习语故事

"white elephant"是一个经济学概念，指的是一项很重要，需要高昂费用支撑，但是最后很难得到巨大效益的资产。

这一习语最早起源于暹罗（泰国），是关于暹罗国王的故事。暹罗国王将一头被认为是"神圣"的白象送给了一位自己不喜欢的大臣，这头大象其实是患有白化病，身体十分脆弱。这位大臣为了照顾这头白象，耗尽了毕生的财产。后来，人们便用"white elephant"表示"华而不实"。

brain drain
人才流失

学以致用

In recent years, there has been a serious brain drain in this region.
近几年,这个地区的人才流失现象十分严重。

The traditional enterprises stand still, leading to the increasingly serious phenomenon of brain drain.
传统企业的故步自封,导致人才流失现象日趋严重。

At present, the brain drain in the travel agency industry has brought great pressure to the management of travel agencies.
目前,旅行社业的人才流失给旅行社的经营管理带来了很大压力。

习语故事

"brain drain"是随着社会的经济发展而形成的习语,意思是指人才的外流,最早出现于第二次世界大战以后。当时,随着美国经济快速发展,很多国家的学生和人才都纷纷去美国的大学深造,并且很多

最后都选择留在了美国，导致很多国家的知识和技术型人才大量流失。"brain drain"中的"brain"在这里指的不是"大脑"，而是比喻那些受过高等教育的人才。

> ghost town
> 被废弃的城镇；"鬼城"

学以致用

After every holiday, the city is like a ghost town. Many young people go to work in other places, and only the old people stay here.
每次假期一过，这座城市便像个"鬼城"，很多年轻人都会去外地工作，只剩下老年人留在这里。

If parking fees in the city center continue to rise, the city center will become a ghost town in the future.
如果市中心的停车费继续涨下去，以后市中心就没人来了。

If something isn't done soon, more shops will close, and the place will become a ghost town.
如果不尽快采取行动，更多的商店将关闭，这个地方将变成一个"鬼城"。

习语故事

　　"ghost town"这一习语起源于 18 至 19 世纪，当时正值美国西部的"淘金热"。"淘金热"时期是美国历史上十分重要的一个阶段，它导致了美国人口的大迁移，甚至开启了美国现代经济发展的进程。当时西部城市的很多小镇都十分繁荣，但是随着淘金活动结束，人们逐渐离开了这些城市。这些城市人口渐渐减少，人们将这些被遗弃的城镇称为"ghost town"。

trailblazer
先驱；开拓者

学以致用

This school is the trailblazer of the model teaching, whose purpose is to help students develop their personal abilities and also develop their intelligence.

这所学校是模型教学的开创者，目的是帮助学生培养个人能力，同时开发学生智力。

We were trailblazers in this industry before, and now we are breaking new ground again.

我们以前是这个行业的开拓者，现在我们要再次开创新的天地。

His company is considered a trailblazer in e-commerce and has led new trends in the market in recent years.

这家公司算是电子商务的开拓者，近几年来引领了市场新潮流。

习语故事

"trailblazer"是在美国西部开发中产生的习语。当时，美国有很多拓荒者到西部开发荒地，他们砍掉树木，开垦土地，建立农场。当时

的拓荒者在小路上每走五十米就用刀砍掉一块树皮，作为给后来人的记号。被砍掉树皮的地方就称为"blaze"，"trial"指的是小路，合起来就是"在小路上砍树皮的人"，后引申为"开拓者"。

习语知识

除了以上随经济发展而来的习语外，还有一些习语也与经济发展有着密切的关系，让我们一起来学习一下吧。

lame duck　不太成功而需要帮助的人（或机构）

这是与金融相关的习语，起源于英国伦敦的股市。在股市当中，人们通常用"lame duck"来喻指无法偿还债务的投资人。后来，这一习语逐渐被广泛使用，来形容那些"失败且需要帮助的人或机构"。

mall rat　喜欢逛街购物的年轻人

这是与商业相关的习语，英美的经济发展带动了商业的快速发展，导致购物中心、大型商场不断涌现。在美国，这些购物中心一般被称为"mall"，而喜欢逛街购物的年轻人就好像商场中的"rat"（老鼠）一样。

趣说科技与习语

科技发展对人们的生活产生了极大的影响，从而也促进了习语文化的发展，很多习语都与科技发明密切相关，让我们一起来看一下吧。

on the same wavelength
观点一致；意气相投

学以致用

The two of them are friends who have known each other since childhood, and

they were on the same wavelength and talked about everything.
他们二人是从小就认识的朋友，一直意气相投，无话不说。

Most problems are a result of misunderstandings where partners are not operating on the same wavelength.
大多数问题都是由误解造成的，是因为合作伙伴的观点不合。

My wife and I sometimes argue about educating our children, but after discussions, we are still on the same wavelength.
我和我的妻子有时也会为了教育孩子的事情争吵，但商量过后，还是会达成一致。

习语故事

"on the same wavelength"是与广播术语相关的习语，指的是观点或意见相投、合得来。"on the same wavelength"中的"wavelength"指的是电台广播节目所使用的波段或者频道，通常情况下，只有双方或多方处于同一波段时，才能相互通信联络。因此，人们常用"on the same wavelength"来表达"观点一致，意气相投"。

pull the plug

暂停；结束

学以致用

The old man decided to pull the plug on spending all that he earned on his children. They should be able to support themselves by their ability.

这位老人决定不再把他挣的钱全都花在他的孩子身上，他们应该凭能力养活自己。

The company pulled the plug on the deal because it was not satisfied with the terms.

该公司取消了这笔交易，因为公司对条款不满意。

Due to poor performance, the boss decided to pull the plug.
由于效益不好,老板决定暂停营业。

习语故事

"pull the plug"是与电力相关的习语,字面意思是"拔掉插头"。这一习语十分生动,拔掉插头后,所有的电力设备都会停止运行。因此,后来人们就用"pull the plug"这一习语表示停止去做某些事情。

blow a fuse
勃然大怒;大发雷霆

学以致用

She's an autocratic person who blows a fuse whenever someone contradicts her point of view.
她是个独断专行的人,只要有人反驳她的观点,她就会大发雷霆。

Because Mark was always distracted in class during this time, resulting in poor test scores this time, his father blew a fuse when he found out.

由于马克这段时间上课总是走神，导致这次考试成绩很差，他父亲知道后勃然大怒。

I broke my mother's favorite vase and my mother blew a fuse.
我把妈妈最喜欢的花瓶打碎了，妈妈勃然大怒。

习语故事

"blow a fuse"的字面意思是"烧断保险丝"。保险丝又称为熔断体，起过载保护作用。众所周知，只要电流异常升高到一定程度，产生的热度极高，达到了保险丝的熔点，就会熔断保险丝。因此，人们常用"blow a fuse"来喻指"十分生气，情绪激动"。

nuts and bolts
具体细节

学以致用

He's more concerned about the nuts and bolts of work.

他更关心工作的具体细节。

Due to the rush of time, many nuts and bolts of this project have not been verified in time, and there may be mistakes.
由于时间仓促，这个项目的很多具体细节还没有来得及核实，可能会出现纰漏。

We are still discussing the nuts and bolts of this project, so there may be a delay of a few days to give you a proposal.
有关这个项目的具体细节我们还在讨论中，因此可能会延迟几天给您提议。

习语故事

"nuts and bolts"是与螺钉和螺母有关的习语，其字面意思就是"螺钉和螺母"。螺钉和螺母是十分重要的科技发明，在螺钉和螺母被发明出来之前，木匠们一直使用木钉将建筑物连接起来，后来螺钉和螺母的发明使得工人的工作变得简单，而且建筑物的连接更加稳固，因此螺钉和螺母被广泛使用。螺钉和螺母虽小，却是家具或者建筑物中最基本的细节构成。因此，人们常用"nuts and bolts"来比喻事情的具体细节。

get someone's wires crossed
误会对方的意思

学以致用

I think we must get his wires crossed. He said to be here before 8:30 in the morning, not 8:30 in the evening.

我想我们一定是误会他的意思了,他说的是早上八点半之前来这里集合,不是晚上八点半。

Did we get the manager's wires crossed? I thought I was going to have a holiday tomorrow, but I still have to go to work.

我们是误会经理的意思了吗?我以为明天要放假,结果还是要上班。

She has always got the teacher's wires crossed. The teacher just wants her to study hard.

她一直都误解了老师的意思,老师只是希望她好好学习。

习语故事

"get someone's wires crossed"是与电力相关的习语,字面意思是"把某人的电线交叉缠绕在一起"。如果电线相互缠绕交叉,电线的端

口接错，那么所在的电力系统将无法正常运行。因此，人们常用"get someone's wires crossed"来表示人们对同一件事情有不同的理解，由于沟通有误，很有可能产生误会，误解对方。

> be firing on all cylinders
> 状态绝佳

学以致用

As his team is gradually firing on all cylinders, Mark believes his team will win.
随着他的球队逐步进入绝佳状态，马克相信他的球队将会取得胜利。

Mary was firing on all cylinders and her sales broke the record this month.
玛丽开足马力工作，这个月的销售额破了纪录。

I drink a cup of coffee every morning so that I can be firing on all cylinders.
我每天早上都要喝一杯咖啡，这样我才能开足马力工作。

习语故事

"be firing on all cylinders"是与汽车相关的习语，其中的"cylinder"是"气缸"的意思，是发动机的重要部件。大多数的汽车中都是有多个气缸的，只有点着所有气缸，发动机才能顺利地运行，汽车的马力才能开到最大。因此，人们常用"be firing on all cylinders"来比喻工作进展十分顺利，或者发挥出了自己最好的状态，就如同汽车开足了所有的马力一样，状态绝佳。

hot off the press
新鲜出炉

学以致用

The singer has a new album hot off the press.

这位歌手有一张专辑即将发行。

As the hot off the press in recent years, distributed optical fiber sensing technology is usually used by students as a research topic.

分布式光纤传感技术作为近年的研究热点，通常会被学生们拿来做研究课题。

The latest chapter of Mary's novel has been hot off the press and the readers are very excited.

玛丽的小说最新一章已经出炉，读者们都十分激动。

习语故事

"hot off the press"是与印刷技术相关的习语，相当于"freshly printed"，也就是"刚刚印刷出来"的意思。人们常用"hot off the press"来比喻新鲜出炉的消息、新闻等，或者用来指刚刚出版的期刊或书籍。

习语知识

除了上述这些习语，还有一些习语也与科技发展有关，让我们一起来学习一下吧。

hit the panic button　　惊慌失措

这一习语与飞行技术有关。在第二次世界大战期间，美国的轰炸机驾驶员在飞机受损时，会按下紧急按钮（panic button）。后来人们便用这一习语来表示惊慌失措，即一个人遇到紧急情况手忙脚乱的样子，就像飞行员在慌乱时按下紧急按钮一样。

reinvent the wheel　　浪费时间做无用功

这一习语与轮子有关。轮子是人类科技史上的一大重要发明，但即使是再伟大的发明，如果再重新发明创造一次，也是在浪费时间做重复工作。因此，人们使用这一习语来表示浪费时间做无用功。

知识活学活用

在学习了与经济和科技相关的习语后，下面来具体运用一下吧。

1. 将下列句子译成中文。

（1）Many things advertised now are white elephants, just to have a good-looking appearance to attract people to buy. In fact, there is no use.

（2）Due to changes in the city's industrial structure, many large-scale heavy industry factories have closed down, and many people have been forced to leave their hometowns to work, which has turned the city into a ghost town.

（3）Mary used to be a typical mall rat hanging around, but since she got a new job, she didn't have the time.

（4）Due to the rain today, the boss pulled the plug on the original team building activity.

（5）The secretary's job is to write down the nuts and bolts of the boss's work in order to assist the boss's work.

（6）After a week of relaxation and rest, everyone is firing on all cylinders to study.

（7）These topics have been studied by previous students, and you just reinvented the wheel.

2. 将下列句子译成英文。

（1）很多小镇由于交通不便，无法吸引年轻人来此落户，反而导致了大量的本地人才流失。

（2）每个行业的开拓者都面临着极大的风险，人们甚至会嘲讽他们所做的事情。

（3）我和我的朋友从小一起长大，我们总是意气相投，无话不谈。

（4）亨利总是在父母出门以后偷偷玩游戏，爸爸发现以后大发雷霆。

（5）我觉得我们都误会了约翰的意思，他并不是想要我们去给他帮忙。

（6）从小父母就告诉我们，遇到危险不要惊慌，一定要尽快冷静下来，想到解决办法。

参考译文

1. 译文如下。

（1）现在广告宣传的东西很多都是华而不实的，只是拥有好看的外表来吸引人去购买，实际上并没有什么用处。

（2）这座城市由于产业结构的变化，很多大型重工业工厂倒闭，很多人被迫离开家乡出去打工，导致这座城市人烟稀少。

（3）玛丽原来很喜欢逛街购物，但是自从她换了新工作以后就没有时间了。

（4）由于今天下雨，老板取消了原定的团建活动。

（5）秘书的工作就是要记下老板工作的具体细节，以便辅助老板的工作。

（6）经过一个星期的放松和休息，大家都准备开足马力学习。

（7）这些课题之前的学生都已经研究过了，你这样再做一遍只是在做无用功。

2. 译文如下。

（1）Many small towns are unable to attract young people to settle here due to inconvenient transportation, which has resulted in a large number of local brain drains.

（2）Trailblazers in every industry are at great risk, and people even make fun of what they do.

（3）My friends and I grew up together, and we always were on the same wavelength and talked about everything.

（4）Henry always secretly played games after his parents went out, and his father blew a fuse when he found out.

（5）I think we all get John's wires crossed. He didn't want us to help him.

（6）Our parents told us from a young age that we should not hit the panic button when faced with danger. We must calm down as soon as possible, and think of a solution.

第四章 CHAPTER 4

孕育于自然环境和风俗习惯中的习语

人们都生活在一定的自然环境中，并形成了一定的风俗习惯，无论是自然环境还是风俗习惯，都对人们的生产生活方式，甚至语言，产生了重要的影响作用。英语中的很多习语源自自然环境和风俗习惯，这些孕育于自然环境和风俗习惯的习语，往往反映着某个地域和民族独一无二的文化。

文化背景解读

自然环境是文化形成的背景和基础,而风俗习惯能够直观地体现某一地区的文化特征。因此,与自然环境和风俗习惯相关的习语比比皆是,这些习语也很好地体现了某一地域和民族的文化特色。

自然环境对习语的影响

自然环境在不同程度上决定着人们的生活方式,影响着人们的思维习惯,因而与自然环境相关的习语能够很好地反映一个民族的文化特色。

英国作为一个岛国，海岸线非常曲折，因此海上运输行业在英国占据了特殊的地位，进而造就了英国的"海洋文化"。在常年的海上生活中，英国人把观察到的现象和积累的经验都应用到了语言中，形成了很多与海相关的习语。例如，英国人在形容人的特点时，往往会用"fish"来表达，"cold fish"就是指"冷漠的人"，而"poor fish"指的是"穷困的人"。这些习语都是英国人在捕鱼的过程中，将日积月累的经验应用到语言中的结果。

而美国地域宽广，拥有丰富的山地、岩石等资源，因此诞生了许多与高山、岩石等相关的习语。这类习语形象生动，在人们的日常生活中应用十分广泛。

风俗习惯对习语的影响

风俗习惯是一种特殊的社会现象，是由社会群体共同创造而成的。每个人从出生起，就会受到其所在社会文化氛围的影响。这些风俗习

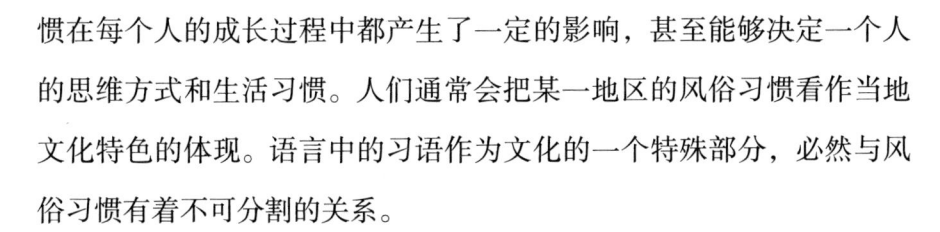

惯在每个人的成长过程中都产生了一定的影响，甚至能够决定一个人的思维方式和生活习惯。人们通常会把某一地区的风俗习惯看作当地文化特色的体现。语言中的习语作为文化的一个特殊部分，必然与风俗习惯有着不可分割的关系。

例如，"as poor as a church mouse"，指的就是"穷困潦倒"，因为西方的教堂中一般不供奉食品，所以教堂里的老鼠是无食可觅的，就会"穷困潦倒，饥肠辘辘"。可见，风俗习惯对于文化的影响极大，而与风俗习惯相关的习语也最能体现民族的文化特征。

趣说自然环境与习语

习语的形成与自然环境有着密切的关系,与自然环境相关的习语有很多,让我们一起来学习一下吧。

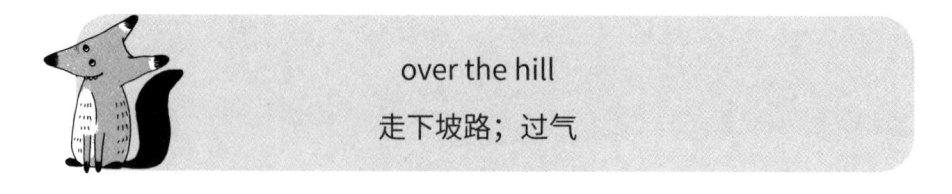

over the hill
走下坡路;过气

学以致用

He thinks that he is over the hill, only to cause trouble for the children.

他认为自己的身体已经每况愈下了，只能给孩子们添麻烦。

This older rugby player proved he is not over the hill after this contest.
这场大赛过后，这位橄榄球老将证明了自己宝刀未老。

I used to think that after the age of 40 all aspects of the body started to be over the hill, but I still feel as youthful as ever.
我曾经认为40岁以后身体各方面已经开始走下坡路了，但我现在感觉我依然像以前一样年轻。

习语故事

"over the hill"是与山有关的习语，字面意思就是"越过山峰"，其实际是指一个人在进入老年时期后，感到各方面都开始走下坡路了。人们常把人生比作一座山峰，"over"在这里就是"越过"的意思，当一个人走过山峰后，就要开始下山了。也就是说，人在越过巅峰以后，就会开始走下坡路。因此，"over the hill"这一习语就是表示人上了年纪后，体力和智力都开始衰退，或过了巅峰期后，就会过气。

the tip of the iceberg
冰山一角

学以致用

What we've seen about damage caused by the earthquake is just the tip of the iceberg.

有关地震所造成的损害,我们看到的只是冰山一角。

As I've discovered, the problems that have been reported to date appear to be only the tip of the iceberg.

正如我发现的那样,迄今为止报告的问题似乎只是冰山一角。

We get about 2,000 complaints every year, but I think that's just the tip of the iceberg.

我们每年大约能收到2000起投诉,但我认为这只是冰山一角。

习语故事

"the tip of the iceberg"是与冰山有关的习语,字面意思就是"冰山一角"。事实上,汉语中的成语"冰山一角"是一个舶来语,这一成语就是来自英语习语"the tip of the iceberg"。

这一习语最早源于北欧，北欧地区纬度较高，气候寒冷，大陆冰川覆盖了整个北欧地区，冰山更是随处可见。北欧人在航海时发现，在海面上看到的部分冰山远远小于水下的部分。因此，后来"the tip of the iceberg"这一习语常被用于表示非常大的事物只显露出了很小的一部分。

> live under a rock
> 与世隔绝

学以致用

This guy lives under a rock. He doesn't know we've changed the head teacher.
这家伙与世隔绝了，他居然不知道我们已经换了班主任。

Have you been living under a rock? Don't you know that Peter and Jane got married?
你是与世隔绝了吗？你不知道皮特和简已经结婚了吗？

I study in the library every day for exams as if I've been lived under a rock.
为了考试我每天都在图书馆学习，好像已经与世隔绝了。

习语故事

"live under a rock"是与岩石有关的习语，字面意思是"生活在岩石下面"。这一习语源自美国，美国的地理特征导致在美国境内有很多岩石地貌，生活在巨大的岩石下面就无法及时接收外界的消息，无法了解时事热点，仿佛"与世隔绝"，因此美国人常用这一习语来形容某人"与世隔绝，消息闭塞"。

between the devil and the deep sea
进退两难

学以致用

You were really between the devil and the deep sea when you had to choose between your career and your relationship.
当你不得不在事业和感情之间做出选择时，真的是进退两难。

Mary found herself between the devil and the deep sea and did not know what to do.
玛丽发现自己陷入了两难的境地，她不知道该怎么做。

Tom was between the devil and the deep sea and he didn't know whether he should stay here or move to another company.

汤姆发现自己已经进退两难,他不知道自己到底是应该留在这里还是跳槽去别的公司。

习语故事

"between the devil and the deep sea"是与海洋有关的习语,字面意思就是"在魔鬼和深海之间"。这一习语源自英国,英国的海岸线绵长,海港水深,具有天然的航海条件,与海相关的习语比比皆是。"deep sea"是"深海"的意思,航海的海员都知道,深海是危险重重的地方,神秘黑暗的深海区域与魔鬼的可怕程度不相上下,"在魔鬼和深海之间"就是指进退两难的处境。于是,英国人就用"between the devil and the deep sea"这一习语来表示"进退维谷"的两难境地。

sea change
巨变；彻底的改变

学以致用

We have just been acquired by a new company. It seems that there would be a sea change in our marketing department.
我们刚被一家新公司收购。我们的市场部似乎要发生翻天覆地的变化。

Since she started working out there has been a sea change in her appearance.
自从她开始锻炼以来，她的外貌发生了巨大的变化。

There was a sea change in his personality after he married his wife.
他和妻子结婚后，他的性格发生了巨大的变化。

习语故事

"sea change"是与海相关的习语，字面意思是指"海的变化"，实际上指的是"彻底的变化，巨大的变化"。"sea change"这一习语源自英国剧作家莎士比亚的戏剧《暴风雨》，剧中的小精灵对青年唱了一首歌，说他父亲因为海难死去了，但随着海的变化，他的父亲也经历了彻底的变化，变成了海里的珊瑚，后来"sea change"也就被用来形容

"彻底的变化"。

由此可以看出，英语中的很多习语与英国的地理特征息息相关，长期生活在海边的英国人，喜欢用海来表达自己的情感。

习语知识

人们往往善于观察身边的自然现象，通过自己的经验总结出相关的习语，以此来生动形象地表达自己的情感。下面让我们一起来学习一下这类习语吧。

up the creek 处境困难；情况不妙

这是与小溪有关的习语，"up the creek"的字面意思是"逆流而上"。众所周知，船只逆流而上时，是十分艰难的，因此"up the creek"这一习语就有了"处境困难"的意思。

water under the bridge 时过境迁；不可改变的事实

这是与自然现象有关的习语，"water under the bridge"的字面意思就是"桥下的流水"。桥下的流水匆匆流走，没有什么办法能阻挡，也无法让流水倒回，因此这一习语被引申为"不可改变的事"。

on the rocks 遭遇危机；濒临破裂；加冰块

这是与岩石相关的习语，"on the rocks"的字面意思是"在岩石上"。这一习语有两层意思，第一层意思是"濒临破裂；遭遇危机"，这与航海过程中触礁的船只有关，触礁的船只会搁浅在海中的岩石上，最后濒临破败，只剩下残骸。另一层意思是"加冰块"，常用于美国口语中，美国人在调酒的时候，一般是先将冰块放在杯中，再倒入酒精饮料，又因为冰块的外形酷似岩石，因此就有了这一说法。

趣说风俗习惯与习语

风俗习惯涉及人们生活的各个方面，包含了饮食习惯、生活方式、社会礼仪以及民俗庆典等，这些风俗习惯产生了很多极具特色的习语，让我们一起来认识一下吧。

bring home the bacon
养家糊口；赚钱谋生

学以致用

I have to go to work because it brings home the bacon.

我不得不去工作，我还要养家糊口呢。

In ancient times, in a family, men brought home the bacon, while women took care of the family at home.

古时候，一个家庭中都是男人出去赚钱谋生，而女人在家照顾家庭。

Because his wife recently suffered a layoff, Mark is so worried that he will have to bring home the bacon, so he was going out to work part-time after getting off work.

因为他的妻子最近遭遇了裁员，马克很是担心，他不得不在下班以后还要再去找一份兼职来养家。

习语故事

"bring home the bacon"是与饮食习惯相关的习语，字面意思是"带培根回家"。"bring home the bacon"中的"bacon"是"培根"的意思，培根是一种烟熏猪肉，是西方人十分喜爱的一种食物。以前在美国乡村有一项"抓猪比赛"，在露天的赛场上，人们需要抓住身上涂满油脂的猪，谁抓住了，谁就能带回家做熏肉。在当时物资匮乏的时期，这一头猪就可以帮助一家人果腹。因此，"bring home the bacon"就被引申为"养家糊口"的意思。

eat one's salt
受某人款待

学以致用

I have eaten my friend's salt for a couple of weeks. I need to hurry up and find a job to stop bothering him.

我的朋友已经款待了我好几周了，我得赶紧找份工作，不能再麻烦他了。

When I ate Mary's salt, I really appreciated her hospitality.

玛丽请我吃饭，我真的很感谢她的盛情款待。

I ate Tom's salt and want to do something for him to thank him for the hospitality.

汤姆请我吃了饭，我想帮他做点什么来感谢他的款待。

习语故事

"eat one's salt"是与拜访习俗有关的习语，字面意思是"吃某人的盐"。这一习语源于阿拉伯习俗，阿拉伯人将食盐奉为神圣的食品。这是因为以前食盐是十分难得的食品，食盐的加工和生产都是十分复杂的，阿拉伯人认为食盐十分珍贵，因此用以款待客人，而客人吃了别人的食盐，就意味着与主人有深厚的交情。后来，人们常用"eat one's salt"来表示"受到款待"。

laugh up one's sleeve
暗暗地笑；窃笑

学以致用

Even though my co-workers seemed to sympathize with me on the surface, I felt like they were all laughing up their sleeves at me for being chewed out by the boss.
尽管我的同事表面上看起来很同情我，但我觉得他们都在暗自嘲笑我被老板训斥了一顿。

I was laughing up my sleeve because her dress was too small for her.

我暗自发笑，因为她的裙子对她而言尺寸过小了。

He cannot help but laugh up his sleeve when he saw someone teasing a puppy on the street.

当他看到有人在街上逗弄小狗时，他忍不住笑了起来。

习语故事

"laugh up one's sleeve"是与生活习惯相关的习语，字面意思是"在袖子里笑"。这个习语源自16世纪上半叶的英国，当时英国的男子衣袖宽大，足以遮住整张脸。出于礼貌，在社交场合如果想要发笑，人们便会用衣袖遮住脸偷偷地笑。于是，"laugh up one's sleeve"就有了"暗暗发笑"的意思。

let one's hair down
放轻松

学以致用

A short vacation allows you to let your hair down and enjoy natural surroundings with a loved one.

一个短暂的假期可以让你放松心情，与爱人一起享受自然。

They finally have the chance to let their hair down and enjoy the evening breeze by the sea.

他们终于有机会放松心情，享受海边的晚风。

The mother had been taking care of her children all night, and when the children finally went to bed, she could let her hair down.

那个妈妈一整晚一直在照顾自己的孩子们，等到孩子们终于睡觉了，她才能放松一下。

习语故事

"let one's hair down"是与生活习俗有关的习语，字面意思是"把头发放下来"。其源自英国早期的生活习惯，早期的英国女性需要将头发往上梳理整齐，无论在什么场合都要保持头发的整齐。只有在自己独处时，才能将头发放下来，放松自己。因此，后来人们就用"let one's hair down"表示"放松下来，放轻松"。

文化解读：趣说英语习语

> give someone the cold shoulder
> 冷落某人；对某人冷淡

学以致用

I always thought that Jenny is my friend, but she gave me the cold shoulder.
我一直当珍妮是我朋友，但是她对我十分冷淡。

Emma gave him the cold shoulder and pretty much ignored him at the party.
艾玛对他十分冷淡，在聚会上几乎不理他。

I fought with my wife, and she is now giving me the cold shoulder.
我和我的妻子吵架了，她现在对我很冷淡。

习语故事

"give someone the cold shoulder"是与待客习俗有关的习语，字面意思是"给某人一块冷肩肉"。"give someone the cold shoulder"中的"cold shoulder"是冷羊肩肉（cold shoulder of mutton）的意思。这一习语与美国人的待客习俗有关，如果客人不受主人欢迎，主人就会拿出冷的羊肩肉来给客人吃。这种肉生硬难嚼，客人吃了就明白了主人的意思。

于是,"give someone the cold shoulder"就有了"冷落某人,对某人冷淡"的意思。

rest on one's laurels
居功自傲;故步自封

学以致用

Even though he has already got the first place, he has never rest on his laurels, but continuously tried to innovate.

即使他已经考到了第一名,他也从来没有骄傲自满,而是不断尝试创新。

Sooner or later, the company will go bankrupt if they keep resting on their laurels.

如果他们继续故步自封,那么公司迟早会破产。

If you rest on your laurels, you will fall behind others.

如果你居功自傲,你就会落后于别人。

习语故事

"rest on one's laurels"是与古希腊人的习俗有关的习语,字面意思

文化解读：趣说英语习语

是"躺在自己的桂冠上"，实际是用来比喻某人满足于自己以往的成就。"rest on one's laurels"中的"laurel"表示"荣誉，成就"。古代希腊人习惯于用月桂树的枝叶做成冠冕，授予那些在竞赛中获得胜利的诗人或者运动员，这一习俗甚至流传至今。一个人如果一直"躺在自己的桂冠上"，满足于自己之前的成就，就是不思进取。因此，"rest on one's laurels"也就引申出了"居功自傲，故步自封"的意思。

习语知识

风俗习惯带有浓重的民族色彩，很多习语都能很好地体现这些风俗习惯，除了上述习语外，还有很多与风俗习惯有关的习语。

bear the palm　获胜；夺魁

这是与古罗马习俗有关的习语，字面意思是"戴上棕榈枝"。在古罗马竞技场上进行格斗一直都是古罗马的习俗，人们习惯于通过格斗来角逐出胜者，胜者则会被授予棕榈枝。因此，"戴上棕榈枝"也就

104

表示这个人获得胜利，夺得了魁首。

smoke the pipe of peace　　言归于好

这是与印第安人习俗有关的习语，字面意思是"抽和平之烟"。北美印第安人喜欢通过请朋友吸烟来表示对外来的朋友的尊敬，如果双方打了架，为了表示和解，便会用一只烟袋轮流吸烟来表示友好。因此，"smoke the pipe of peace"也就有了"和解"的意思。

take one's bread out of someone's mouth　　夺人生计

这是与饮食习惯有关的习语，字面意思是"从别人口中抢走了面包"。英美国家由于地理环境和生活习惯的原因，主要以谷类作物，如小麦、大麦和燕麦等食物作为主食，面包便成为英美国家人民的主食，因此人们通常会用面包来比喻"生计"。如果一个人从别人嘴里抢走面包，那么就意味着这个人夺走了别人的生计。

take off one's hat to someone　　向某人致敬

这是与社交习俗有关的习语，字面意思是"对着某人脱帽"。中世纪的英国人十分流行戴帽子，一般在社交场合与他人打招呼时，或是见到别人想要表示尊重时，都会脱帽来示意。后来，"take off one's hat to someone"这一习语也就引申为"向某人致敬"。

知识活学活用

在学习了这么多有关自然环境和风俗习惯的习语后,下面一起来运用一下吧。

1. 将下列句子译成中文。

(1) Once you start to be over the hill in all aspects of your body, you must pay attention to your schedule and don't stay up late.

(2) A recent report on the hidden risks of a big belly found that if you have a big belly, your chances of developing dementia in later life roughly double. However, this may be just the tip of the iceberg of the consequences of obesity.

（3）I'm caught between the devil and the deep sea. If I choose now to go on vacation, I may get fired, but if I don't go, my girlfriend may leave me.

（4）The couple and their three children were forced to move into the rental property because they had sold their original home and they were up the creek without a paddle.

（5）What's past is past and there's no use crying about water under the bridge.

（6）Mommy needs to be gainfully employed so that she can bring home the bacon.

（7）She had forgotten how great it felt to just let her hair down and go out and enjoy the trip with her lover.

（8）We can't rest on our laurels; we should continue to work very hard to achieve better results.

（9）Jane bore the palm in all she attempted and was acknowledged supreme among her school fellows.

（10）As long as we work hard and keep improving our skills, we will not be afraid of others taking the bread out of our mouths.

2. 将下列句子译成英文。

（1）在特效照片编辑方面，这篇文章中提到的功能只是冰山一角。

（2）我们一定要多与人交流，不能过与世隔绝的生活。

（3）玛丽的母亲三年前得了重病，经过这场变故，玛丽成熟了很多，每天早上四点起床照顾母亲。

（4）自从我听说凯丽一直在背后跟别人说我的坏话，我和她的关系就一直岌岌可危。

（5）由于我出差的地方距离我朋友家很近，他知道了以后已经款待了我好多天了。

（6）我在采访他的时候，他一直在发出窃笑。我觉得他很不尊重我。

（7）人们选择去那里度假，放松心情，尽情享受。

（8）前一天舞会上她表现得对我很感兴趣，第二天却对我冷淡了。

（9）今天的会场来了许多优秀的学者和专家，我应该向他们致敬。

参考译文

1. 译文如下。

（1）一旦你的身体各方面开始走下坡路了，就一定要注意作息规律，不要再熬夜了。

（2）近期关于大肚腩隐藏风险的一项报告指出，如果你有大肚腩，那么在晚年患上痴呆症的概率大概要增加两倍。不过，这也许只是肥胖所带来恶果的冰山一角。

（3）我陷入了进退两难的境地，如果我现在选择去度假，我可能会被解雇，但如果我不去，我的女朋友可能会离开我。

（4）这对夫妇和他们的三个孩子被迫搬进了出租房，因为他们已经把原来的房子卖掉了，他们现在处境艰难。

（5）过去的事情已经过去了，时过境迁再痛哭也无用。

（6）妈妈需要出去工作，这样她才能养家糊口。

（7）她已经忘记了放松下来、与爱人一起出去享受旅行的感觉有多棒了。

（8）我们不能居功自傲，我们应该继续努力工作，取得更好的成绩。

（9）简在她参加的比赛中一直都是胜者，她是同学们公认的好学生。

（10）只要我们尽心尽力地工作，不断地精进自己的技艺，就不怕别人抢饭碗。

2. 译文如下。

（1）The features in this article are merely the tip of the iceberg when it comes to special effects in photo editing.

（2）We must communicate with people more and not live under a rock.

（3）Mary's mother was seriously ill three years ago. After this sea change, Mary has matured a lot and gets up at four every morning to take care of her mother.

（4）My relationship with kelly has been on the rocks ever since I heard that she has been talking bad about me behind my back.

（5）Since the location of my business trip is close to my friend's house, I ate his salt in his house for a few days for dinner after he found out.

（6）When I interviewed him, he kept laughing up his sleeve. I think he is very disrespectful to me.

（7）People choose to go there on holiday to let their hair down and enjoy themselves.

（8）She showed interest in me at the dance the day before, but the next day she gave me the cold shoulder.

（9）Many excellent scholars and experts have come to today's meeting. I should take off my hat to them.

第五章 CHAPTER 5

根植于动物与植物的习语

人与动物和植物的关系可以追溯到远古时代，动物和植物都是人类赖以生存的物质基础，动植物与人类社会的关系密不可分。因此，语言中存在着大量以动植物为喻体的习语，动植物的象征意义反映了人们数千年的生活经验。与动物和植物相关的习语不胜枚举，许多习语沿用至今。

文化背景解读

与动物和植物相关的习语蕴含着大量的文化信息,这些习语形象生动,特色鲜明,大大丰富了英语语言。

动物习语丰富多样

动物最初作为人类的捕猎对象,是为人类提供能量的物质基础。但随着人类驯服和饲养动物后,动物与人类社会的关系逐渐密切。人类在与动物接触的过程中,通过观察动物的生活习性、外形特征等,

创造了许多与动物相关的习语，使得动物习语丰富多样。

例如，狗是人类最好的朋友，与人类社会的关系也最为密切。在西方，人们认为狗是最忠诚的动物，因此"as faithful as a dog"就可以用来形容一个人的忠心耿耿。这类与动物相关的习语生动地表达了人们的思想和感情，寓意深远。

在英语习语中出现的动物有数百种，包括陆地动物、飞禽和昆虫等。这些习语充分体现了人们的想象力，也表达了各种各样的思想、感情以及对客观世界的认识，丰富了语言文化。

植物习语寓意深刻

植物对语言文化的影响不言而喻，与植物有关的习语往往会折射出一个民族的文化特色，其象征意义和联想意义都十分丰富。与植物有关的习语，往往蕴含着丰富的精神文化。植物所蕴含的意义不仅能够展现民族文化，还会影响人们的审美意识。

例如，玫瑰在西方文化中占有举足轻重的地位。玫瑰是爱神的化身，甚至西方的诗人会专门为歌颂玫瑰而创作诗集。玫瑰还对西方宗教有着特殊的意义，与中国的莲花有着异曲同工之妙。由此可见，植物蕴含着浓郁的文化气息，能够展现出文化的特色。

趣说动物与习语

与动物相关的习语往往生动有趣,暗含着动物的外形特征和生活习性,下面就让我们一起来学习一下吧。

butterflies in one's stomach
忐忑不安

学以致用

I'm hosting the big event next week. I have butterflies in my stomach right now.

下周我要主持这项大型活动，现在心里有些忐忑不安。

The first time I went on stage I had butterflies in my stomach.
我第一次上台的时候，心里忐忑不安。

Mary had butterflies in her stomach at the beginning of the interview, but she soon relaxed once she realized how down-to-earth Mr. Harold was.
玛丽在面试开始时还有点紧张，但当她意识到哈罗德先生是一位十分随和的人时，便很快就放松下来了。

习语故事

"butterflies in one's stomach"是关于蝴蝶的习语，字面意思就是"肚子里有很多蝴蝶"。这是一种十分生动的表达，肚子里有很多蝴蝶在飞，形象地形容了一种持续不断的恐惧、紧张、忧虑的心情，因此也就有了"忐忑不安，心里七上八下"的意思。

cast pearls before swine
对牛弹琴

学以致用

Even if we repeat these points to them a hundred times, we would only be casting pearls before swine.

即使我们给他们重复一百次，也只是对牛弹琴。

Josie always likes to do things according to her own ideas, and she is very stubborn, and reasoning with her is like casting pearls before swine.

乔西总是喜欢按照自己的想法来做事，而且她这个人固执得很，跟她讲道理简直是对牛弹琴。

The teacher severely criticized Mark because he was late for class every time. The teacher reminded him many times, but every time it was like casting pearls before swine.

老师严厉地批评了马克，因为他每次上课都迟到，老师提醒了他很多次，但每次都像对牛弹琴。

习语故事

"cast pearls before swine"是与猪有关的习语，"swine"是"pig"的书面语，指的是"猪"，整个习语的字面意思是"将珍珠丢到猪的面前"。这个习语与汉语中的"对牛弹琴"含义相同，都有"不识好意"的意思。该习语十分生动和贴切，所以一直被沿用至今。

wild goose chase
徒劳无功；白费力气

学以致用

Once you start doing a lot of things, you must stick to it, otherwise everything you do will be on a wild goose chase.

很多事情你一旦开始做了，就一定要坚持下去，否则你所做的一切将是徒劳无功的。

John looking for his lost phone may be on a wild goose chase.

约翰正在找他丢失的手机，这可能是白费力气。

It turns out that my brother took my car keys. I had been on a wild goose chase this whole morning searching them in the entire house.

原来我哥哥拿走了我的车钥匙，我还白费力气在屋子里找了一上午。

习语故事

"wild goose chase"是与鹅相关的习语，字面意思是"追逐一只鹅"。这一习语被解释为"白费力气"，其实和赛马运动相关。

早在16世纪，赛马运动是在茂密的森林里进行的，比赛规定，所

有的赛马应该要紧追一匹"头马",但"头马"性情暴烈,奔跑时往往没有规律的路线,因此很多骑士在追逐"头马"的过程中都迷失了路线,最后也无法到达终点。

于是,人们认为这种追逐"头马"的行为,往往是一种"白费力气"的行为。因这种追逐"头马"的阵形与鹅群类似,鹅群一般都会有一只"领航"的,所以当时的人们就戏称赛马为"wild goose chase"。后来,"wild goose chase"这一习语就有了"徒劳无功,白费力气"的意思。

the world is one's oyster
随心所欲

学以致用

When you're young, you think the world is your oyster.
在你年轻的时候,你认为世界任你驰骋。

I asked my mom that if she thought the world was my oyster, why she wouldn't let me travel to Europe this summer.
我问妈妈,既然她说我可以随心所欲,为什么她不能让我今年夏天去欧洲旅游。

You are young and well educated. Don't be sad. The world is your oyster.

你既年轻又受过良好的教育,别难过,这世界是属于你的。

习语故事

"the world is one's oyster"是有关牡蛎的习语,字面意思就是"这世界是某人的牡蛎"。这个习语最早是起源于莎士比亚的戏剧《温莎的风流妇人》(*The Merry Wives of Windsor*)。"the world is one's oyster"中的"oyster"是牡蛎的意思,牡蛎可以孕育名贵的珍珠,在西方文化中具有"幸运、机遇"的含义。将世界比喻成牡蛎,你可以用刀子将它撬开,可以任意掌握它的一切。因此,"the world is one's oyster"就有了"随心所欲,这世界任你掌控"的意思。这是一句十分激励人心的习语,在情绪低落时,可以说一句"the world is my oyster"。

have/put/get one's ducks in a row
把事情安排得井井有条

学以致用

You can't get this public fund-raising campaign going if you don't have your ducks in a row.

如果你不把事情都安排妥当，这次的公共筹款就无法开展。

The crew worked together to get our ducks in a row as we headed back to the ship.
我们回到船上时，船员们已经安排好了一切。

We have an event planned, so we have to get all our ducks in a row first.
我们规划了一个活动，所以我们必须先把所有事情都安排妥当。

习语故事

"have/put/get one's ducks in a row"是与鸭子有关的习语，其字面意思是"把鸭子排成一排"。鸭子在行走的过程中，走在最前面的鸭子被称作头鸭，其余的鸭子都跟随头鸭自动排成一排，看起来仿佛是头鸭为后面的鸭子安排好了顺序。后来，人们根据鸭子的这种习性，将"have/put/get one's ducks in a row"延伸为"把事情安排妥当"。

shooting fish in a barrel
易如反掌；轻而易举

学以致用

Becoming a good teacher isn't like shooting fish in a barrel. It takes a lot of effort and preparation.

想要成为一名优秀的教师可不是一件容易的事，需要做很多努力和准备。

For my exam I was really nervous and worried that it would be too difficult for me, but it was actually as easy as shooting fish in a barrel!

考试时，我真的很紧张，担心考试对我来说太难了，但实际上简直是手到擒来！

The teacher once said that writing a good essay is not like shooting fish in a barrel. You must read a lot of books and pay attention to record everything that happens in your daily life.

老师曾经说过，写好文章可不是一件简单的事情，一定要阅读大量的书籍，还要留意记录日常生活中发生的每一件事。

习语故事

"shooting fish in a barrel"是与鱼有关的习语，字面意思就是"射杀桶里的鱼"。从字面意思就很容易理解，鱼已经在桶中，那么射杀它们简直是易如反掌的事情。该习语与汉语中的"瓮中捉鳖"有异曲同工之妙，都十分生动形象。

the lion's share
最大的一份；最大的份额

学以致用

Although she always sits there quietly, she always got the lion's share of attention from her teachers because of her excellent academic performance.
虽然她总是很安静地坐在那里，但由于她学习成绩优异，她总是能得到老师最多的关注。

William has been appointed administrative manager, which means he will take on the lion's share of administrative work in the company.
威廉被任命为行政经理，这意味着他将要承担公司里更多的行政工作。

My older brother always got the lion's share of the french fries when we were younger.
我们小时候，我哥哥吃的那份薯条总是最多的。

习语故事

"the lion's share"是关于狮子的习语，字面意思就是"狮子那份"。狮子与其他野兽一起打猎后，分配战利品的时候，狮子总是依仗自己

的威严，占据最多的那份，而其他的动物只能得到很少的一部分。后来，人们就将"the lion's share"引申为"最大的一份"。

习语知识

与动物相关的习语还有很多，有些也十分经典，让我们一起来看一下吧。

let the cat out of the bag　泄露秘密；露出马脚

该习语与猫有关，字面意思是"把猫从口袋里放出来"，实际指的是"露出马脚，泄露秘密"。古代英国的集市上，有些奸诈的商人会把小猫放在口袋里冒充小猪仔卖给顾客，如果买主不打开袋子看一下的话，就会把小猫当成小猪买回去。但如果"把猫从口袋里放出来"，就会暴露商人的秘密，让他们露出马脚。

watch something or someone like a hawk　紧盯某人/某事

该习语与鹰有关，字面意思是"像鹰一样看着某人/某事"。众所周知，鹰的眼睛十分锐利，可以在高空中紧盯猎物。因此，像鹰一样看着某人/某事，就是"紧盯着某人/某事"。

mad as a hornet　怒不可遏

该习语与黄蜂有关，其字面意思是"如黄蜂一样愤怒"。黄蜂的雌蜂尾端有长而粗的螫针，黄蜂的进攻性极强，而且尾针有毒。如果遇到攻击，黄蜂会十分愤怒，群起而攻之。因此，人们根据它们的这种习性，将"mad as a hornet"引申为"怒不可遏"。

趣说植物与习语

与植物相关的习语象征意义和联想意义都十分丰富,往往带有很浓郁的文化特色,下面就让我们一起来学习一下吧。

everything's coming up roses
一切进展顺利

学以致用

She became a college student and has just won a scholarship. Everything in her life is coming up roses.

她成了一名大学生,又刚刚获得奖学金,她生活中的一切都变得美好起来。

Everything was coming up roses and there was nothing to worry about.

一切都进展顺利,没什么好担心的。

He told us the economy of company was in great shape, and everything was coming up roses.

他告诉我们公司的经济状况良好,一起都进展顺利。

习语故事

"everything's coming up roses"是与玫瑰相关的习语,字面意思是"一切冒出了玫瑰花",实际意思是"一切进展顺利"。在西方文化中,玫瑰是幸运、美好的象征,因此"everything's coming up roses"就是指"每件事都是美好幸运的",也就有了"一切进展顺利"的意思。

fresh as a daisy
精神焕发

学以致用

I was in bed by 8: 30 pm last night and this morning awoke fresh as a daisy, ready to face the day shift.

我昨天晚上八点半就上床睡觉了，今天早上醒来时精神焕发，准备迎接白天的工作。

I think I look exhausted at the moment but he looked fresh as a daisy.

我觉得那时我看起来很疲惫，而他看着神采奕奕。

I went on a mountain vacation last week and got plenty of sleep every day, so I'm fresh as a daisy this week.

我上周去了山区度假，每天睡眠都很充足，因此这周我精神饱满。

习语故事

"fresh as a daisy"是与雏菊有关的习语，字面意思是"像雏菊一样充满朝气"。"fresh as a daisy"中的"daisy"指的是"雏菊"，雏菊是菊花的一种，小小的花瓣，在夜间会将花瓣卷起来，清晨时绽放。后来，人们便用"fresh as a daisy"来形容一个人精神饱满，充满活力。

gild the lily
画蛇添足；多此一举

学以致用

You do not need to add this argument at the end of this article. It is gilding the lily.

你的这篇文章没必要在最后添加这一段议论，这是多此一举。

He has made it clear that this work is already perfect and to add anything else is to gild the lily.

他明确表示，这件作品已经很完美了，再加任何东西都是画蛇添足。

The design of this dress is already perfect. Don't add anything to it at all. It would just be gilding the lily.

这件衣服的设计已经十分完美了，不要添加任何内容，那只会是多此一举。

习语故事

"gild the lily"是与百合花有关的习语，字面意思就是"给百合花镀金"。在西方文化中，人们认为百合花是最纯洁干净的，给百合花镀

金无异于"画蛇添足",反而破坏了百合花的纯洁和美好。因此,"gild the lily"也就引申为"画蛇添足,多此一举"的意思了。

shrinking violet
害羞；腼腆

学以致用

There are no shrinking violets in our class. Everyone has the courage to express their opinions.
我们班里没有羞怯的人,每个人都勇于表达自己的观点。

Girls were no shrinking violets when they attended the dance.
姑娘们在参加舞会的时候,没有表现出害羞腼腆。

I am not exactly a shrinking violet, but I don't have the courage to say those confessions you said to her.
我虽然不是个腼腆的人,但是你对她说的那些表白的话,我是没有勇气说出来的。

习语故事

"shrinking violet"是与紫罗兰有关的习语,字面意思是"害羞的

紫罗兰"。紫罗兰这种花通常会在角落里独自开放，因此人们赋予了紫罗兰害羞的特征，常常用紫罗兰来形容一个人羞涩腼腆。这一习语最早源于英国作家李·亨特的文章，后来被广泛应用。

grasp at straws
抓住救命稻草

学以致用

He saw Mike, who had learned taekwondo, and he seemed to be desperately grasping at straws.

他看到了学过跆拳道的麦克，他似乎想要拼命地抓住麦克这根救命稻草。

He only started reading the night before the exam, just trying to grasp at straws.

他在考试前一天晚上才开始看书，只不过是想抓住救命稻草。

She desperately grabs a floating board after falling into the water, like grasping at a straw.

她掉进水里后，拼命地抓住了一块浮板，就像是抓住救命稻草一般。

习语故事

"grasp at straws"是与稻草有关的习语,该习语的字面意思是"抓住稻草",实际意思与汉语中的"抓住救命稻草"一样。"grasp at straws"一般用于形容在紧张的情况下,人们都会拼命寻找一种方法,试图能够挽回局面。

spill the beans
泄露秘密

学以致用

If I spill the beans, will you promise not to tell anyone else?
如果我把这个秘密告诉你,你能保证不告诉别人吗?

We secretly arranged a birthday party for a colleague and wanted to surprise him, but Mary accidentally spilled the beans to him about it.
我们偷偷地为同事安排了一个生日聚会,想要给他一个惊喜,但玛丽不小心把这件事告诉了他。

Henry's family conditions are not very good. He has never liked to talk about his family, but Ben accidentally spilled the beans, which made Henry very unhappy.

亨利的家庭条件不太好,他一直不喜欢谈论自己的家庭,但是本不小心泄露了这个秘密,导致亨利很不开心。

习语故事

"spill the beans"是与豆子有关的习语,字面意思是"倒豆子"。在古希腊时期,一些社团在招收社员的时候会请社员投票,每位社员都会往瓶子里放豆子来表示支持还是反对,如果瓶子倒了,豆子掉出来,那么匿名投票的结果就会泄露出来。因此,后来人们便用"spill the beans"表示"泄露秘密"。

习语知识

英语中与植物相关的习语还有很多,除了上面介绍的这些,还有一些也十分经典,让我们一起来了解一下吧。

shake like a leaf 因紧张或害怕而战栗

这是与树叶有关的习语,字面意思就是"抖得像树叶"。风起时,树叶会随着风摇摆,沙沙作响。用抖动的树叶来形容一个人因害怕而战栗,十分生动形象。

olive branch 和解;示好

这是与橄榄相关的习语,字面意思就是我们熟悉的"橄榄枝"。

这一习语也与古希腊神话有关，海神波塞冬和女神雅典娜因以谁的名字来命名阿提卡半岛上的一座城市而发生冲突，评判者决定谁能给人民带来珍贵的礼物，谁就是胜者。雅典娜选择把尖锐的兵器变成了一株橄榄树，结束这场斗争。雅典娜因给人们带来了和平而赢得了胜利。因此，"橄榄枝"也就成了和平的象征。"olive branch"也就被引申出了"和解，示好"的意思。

through the grapevine　道听途说

这是与葡萄藤相关的习语，字面意思是"经过葡萄藤"，实际意思是"道听途说"。该习语最早见于电报兴起的时期，当时很多公司安装了电报机，拉起了电线。当时的工人并不够专业，拉起的电线往往缠绕在一起，远远看上去就像一根葡萄藤一样。后来在美国南北战争时期，交战双方都会通过电报发送假情报来迷惑对方。因此，"through the grapevine"就有了"小道消息"的意思，同时延伸出了"道听途说"的意思。

知识活学活用

在学习了这么多有关动物和植物的习语后，一起来运用一下吧。

1. 将下列句子译成中文。

（1）As Friday rehearsal rolled around, I had butterflies in my stomach.

（2）He gave us the wrong directions to the station and that led us off on a wild goose chase.

（3）He now knows the world is his oyster and that he can do more things he wants to do.

（4）My son is upset that his brother got the lion's share of the cake but I explained because it was his birthday.

（5）You are well prepared and your resume is great. I am sure that it will come up roses for you. You will get the job.

（6）What you said just now is perfect, but you added the last sentence, which is just gilding the lily.

（7）Everyone knows that I am not a shrinking violet. I like to stand on the stage and express my views.

（8）I couldn't answer the teacher's question. I looked at my friend and tried to grasp at straws.

（9）We have offered the olive branch on many occasions, only to have it cut away.

2. 将下列句子译成英文。

（1）给那些不懂音乐的人听这些歌，简直是对牛弹琴。

（2）在开始新工作之前，我需要把所有的事情都安排妥当。

（3）她是个优秀的技工。对她来说，换轮胎简直是易如反掌。

（4）你可以带妹妹去游泳，但是一定盯紧了她，她游泳不是很好。

（5）他做事总是拖拖拉拉，导致这次耽误了重要的事，他母亲得知这件事后非常生气。

（6）我昨晚睡了个好觉，今天精神抖擞。

（7）不要告诉莎拉任何秘密，因为她根本保守不住秘密。

参考译文

1. 译文如下。

（1）随着周五彩排的临近，我心里十分紧张。

（2）他给我们指的去车站的路是错误的，让我们白费了一番力气。

（3）他现在知道这世界任他驰骋，他可以做更多他想做的事情。

（4）我儿子对他哥哥分到了最大块的蛋糕表示不满，但我跟他解释，今天是哥哥的生日。

（5）你准备得很好，简历也很棒。我相信一切都会顺利的，你会得到这份工作的。

（6）你刚才已经说得很好了，但你说的最后一句话真是画蛇添足。

（7）所有人都知道我不是一个羞涩的人。我喜欢站在舞台上表达我的观点。

（8）我回答不上来老师的问题，我把目光投向我的朋友，试图抓住他这根救命稻草。

（9）我们曾多次示好，但是都被拒绝了。

2. 译文如下。

（1）To make those who don't understand music listen to these songs is like casting pearls before swine.

（2）I need to have all my ducks in a row before starting any new job.

（3）She's a good mechanic. Changing a tire is like shooting fish in a barrel for her.

（4）You can take your little sister swimming, but please, watch her like a hawk. She isn't a good swimmer.

（5）He is always procrastinating in doing things, which has led to the delay of important things this time and his mother was as mad as a hornet when she learned about it.

（6）I had a great night's sleep last night and am fresh as a daisy today.

（7）Don't tell Sarah anything confidential because she's incapable of not spilling the beans.

第六章 CHAPTER 6

妙趣横生的颜色与地名习语

颜色和地名都与文化有着密切的关系。人们通常会选择用颜色来表现心理,颜色甚至会反映出人们的价值取向。而地名从命名开始就有着浓郁的文化特色,可以反映当地的地理、历史、风俗等文化现象。英语中有很多习语都源自颜色和地名,这些习语生动形象,寓意深刻,反映着西方文化的特色。

文化背景解读

颜色和地名与文化的关系密不可分,很多颜色和地名往往被赋予了不同的文化内涵。对于颜色而言,每种颜色都有着不同的寓意,而且这些寓意大多可以反映人们的心理状态。对于地名而言,地名有着显著的文化特点,大多数地名命名的背后都有很多故事。

颜色对习语的影响

颜色是一种视觉感受,一般来讲,人们对于颜色的感知都是一致的。但颜色与各民族的风土人情、思维方式等有着密不可分的关系,

人们总是会按照自己的思维方式和价值观念来描绘颜色，赋予颜色以丰富的内涵。

例如，西方人通常认为绿色是不健康的颜色，西方人习惯用绿色来描述一个人面色不佳、情绪不好。人们通常还会认为黑色是不祥之色，象征着邪恶，因此"black market"也就有了"非法"的含义。有人还会认为黄色是凶兆之色，认为黄色是不忠诚的象征。可见，颜色被赋予的意义极为丰富，每种颜色都有着特殊的象征意义。

地名对习语的影响

地名不仅是一个名称，还是一种文化现象，反映着民族的地理、语言、文化、风俗以及历史事件等。与地名相关的英语习语在日常用语中十分常见。

比如纽卡斯尔（Newcastle），它是英格兰东北部的一座港口城市，一直都是英国的产煤中心。因此，便衍生出"carry coals to Newcastle"这一习语，指的就是将煤炭运往纽卡斯尔，比喻"白费力气，做无用之功"。

地名往往能因此地发生的历史事件和文化特色给人们留下深刻的印象，同时被人们融入语言当中，进而形成脍炙人口的习语，并被人们广泛使用。

趣说颜色与习语

与颜色相关的习语往往形象鲜明,生动活泼。那么,就让我们一起来认识一下这些习语吧。

paint the town red
狂欢作乐

学以致用

Jack finally reached his annual performance goal tonight, and he invited everyone to paints the town red.

杰克今晚终于达成年度的业绩目标,他请大家一起去狂欢一晚。

We came to this restaurant and painted the town red to celebrate my friend's birthday.

我们为了庆祝我朋友的生日,来到这家饭店狂欢痛饮。

On the last night of the trip, we planned to enjoy a comfortable dinner in the resort house and then go to the room to paint the town red.

旅行最后一晚,我们计划在度假屋里享受舒适的晚餐,然后回到房间开怀痛饮。

习语故事

"paint the town red"是与红色有关的习语,字面意思是"将城镇涂成红色",实际上指的是"狂欢作乐,开怀畅饮"。这一习语的产生据说与英国的沃特福德侯爵有关,他和朋友们在城镇里喝酒,这群人喝醉后,开始狂欢作乐,给当地造成了诸多损失,不仅打翻了花盆,打碎了玻璃,还用红漆把几栋建筑都涂成了红色。后来,人们就用"paint the town red"表示"狂欢作乐"。

be tickled pink
眉开眼笑

学以致用

Seeing the old friend coming, he was immediately tickled pink, while he stretched out his hand to invite the old friend to his house.

看到老朋友来了,他马上眉开眼笑,边笑边伸出手把老朋友往家里请。

Everyone was tickled pink watching the little ballerinas try to dance at the recital.

看着小芭蕾舞演员在独奏会上跳舞,大家都眉开眼笑的。

I'm tickled pink to hear that my sister was admitted to college.

听到妹妹考上了大学,我真的很高兴。

习语故事

"be tickled pink"是与粉色相关的习语,其中的"tickle"是"挠痒痒"的意思。这一习语从字面意思理解,就是挠痒痒的时候,脸会变红。当人被挠痒痒的时候,会觉得很痒,难以忍受,就会发笑,脸就会憋红。后来,"be tickled pink"也就被引申为"非常开心,眉

开眼笑"。

on a silver platter
唾手可得

学以致用

She has never had to work a day in her life. Her parents hand her everything on a silver platter.

她一生中从未工作过一天,有了她父母,所有的东西她都唾手可得。

Maybe it's because they were too complacent and handed over the trophy that was handed on a silver platter.

可能是因为他们太得意忘形了,把本来唾手可得的奖杯拱手让给他人了。

With this opportunity that was handed on a silver platter, it was hard for Mark to resist the temptation.

眼前这个机会唾手可得,马克很难禁得住诱惑。

习语故事

"on a silver platter"是与银色有关的习语,"on a silver platter"的字面意思是"放在银盘子上"。这一习语主要说的是银器十分珍贵,只有有钱人才能使用。在以前,有钱人一般都不需要自己亲自去做什么事情,所要的东西基本都是由管家放在银盘子里,然后拿到他们的面前。因此,"on a silver platter"这一习语渐渐地就有了"唾手可得"的意思。后来,这一习语还延伸出了"不劳而获"的意思。

have a heart of gold
心地善良

学以致用

Your donation to the charity shows that you really have a heart of gold.
你能为慈善机构捐款,表明你真的是一个心地善良的人。

My friend has a heart of gold. Whenever I need her help, she always lends a helping hand.
我的朋友有一颗善良的心,每当我需要她的帮助时,她总是会伸出援助之手。

That doctor has a heart of gold and he was always willing to listen to others talk about his pain, and he would always call them after treatment to remind them to rest.

那位医生心地善良，他总是愿意倾听病人诉说自己的痛苦，治疗后也总会打电话给他们，提醒他们多多休息。

习语故事

"have a heart of gold"是与金色有关的习语，其字面意思是"有一颗金色的心"。"gold"除了有"金色"的意思外，还有"金子"的意思。金子是一种十分贵重的金属，用它来修饰"heart"，可以表示内心的善良。后来，"have a heart of gold"这一习语便用来表示一个人心地善良、慷慨大度、品德高尚。

blue blood
出身名门

学以致用

It is written in this novel that Mark's family was of the purest blue blood, so since his birth, he has been the owner of these three manors.

这本小说中写道,马克的家族是真正出身名门的贵族,所以从他一出生,他就是这三个庄园的主人。

Although he came from the family of blue blood, he still insisted on starting a business on his own.
虽然他出身显赫,但他仍坚持靠自己的力量开创事业。

In both films, she played the role of the well-heeled, blue blood heiress.
在这两部电影中,她都扮演了富有的、出身名门的女继承人的角色。

习语故事

"blue blood"是与蓝色有关的习语,其字面意思是"蓝血"。这一习语最早源于西班牙王室,西班牙王室和贵族的祖先是西哥特人,他们的肌肤雪白,蓝色的静脉血管清晰可见,因此他们称自己为"blue blood"。后来,这一习语也慢慢延伸到了各欧洲贵族中,用来与平民做区别。现在,"blue blood"也多用于象征奢华高贵的品牌。

(as) white as a sheet
面色惨白

学以致用

When he witnessed the accident, he went as white as a sheet, which later affected his driver's license test.

他目睹车祸的发生，当时吓得面色惨白，以至于后来对他考驾照都有影响。

Mark dressed in black, looking thin as a rake and white as a sheet.

马克穿着黑色的衣服，瘦得像个靶子，面色惨白。

I woke up this morning white as a sheet after staying up late last night.

昨晚熬夜后，我今天早上醒来时脸色苍白。

习语故事

"(as) white as a sheet"是与白色有关的习语，其字面意思为"像纸一样白"。这一习语多是用来形容人受到惊吓后，面色吓得惨白。大多数西方人的皮肤十分白皙，无论受到什么惊吓，面色变化都不太明显。于是，西方人常常会通过比喻的方式来形象地描述面色的变化。这一习语还有另一个表达方式，即"(as) white as a ghost"，都是指的"面如纸色，毫无血色"。

习语知识

除了上述习语，还有很多习语与颜色相关，让我们一起来学习一下吧。

once in a blue moon　千载难逢

"once in a blue moon"中的"blue moon"指的并不是"蓝月亮"，而是一种天文现象，指的是一个月中的第二次满月，这种情况是极为罕见的，可以称得上是"千载难逢，百年难遇"，因此"once in a blue moon"就有了"千载难逢"的意思。

as black as a sweep　肮脏不堪

"as black as a sweep"中的"sweep"在这里不是"打扫"的意思，而是指"烟囱清洁工"，整个习语的字面意思是"和烟囱清洁工一样黑"。在西方的家庭建筑中，一般都会有壁炉，壁炉上连着烟囱，这个时候就需要烟囱清洁工来疏通烟囱。烟囱清洁工干完活后，身上总是肮脏不堪。因此，"as black as a sweep"常用来表示一个人身上"非常脏"。

趣说地名与习语

西方有些地名与当地的风土文化密不可分,因此便诞生了许多与地名相关的习语,让我们一起来学习一下吧。

not for all the tea in China
无论如何都不

学以致用

I wouldn't hang out with her again for all the tea in China. She is late every time!

我无论如何都不会再和她出去玩了，她每次都会迟到！

He is my friend. I believe in his character. I would never believe him to do such a dirty thing for all the tea in China.

他是我的朋友，我相信他的人品，我无论如何都不会相信他会做那样龌龊的事情。

I would not for all the tea in China help you with your homework anyway. It's cheating the teacher.

我无论如何都不会帮你写作业，这是欺骗老师的行为。

习语故事

"not for all the tea in China"是与中国相关的习语，这一习语源自19世纪，当时中国所盛产的茶叶在西方属于"奢侈品"。西方人都会用高价来购买茶叶，甚至会献上自己国家的珍宝只为求得中国的茶叶。

尤其是在英国，英国人对中国茶叶的喜爱，简直到了痴迷的程度。"not for all the tea in China"按字面理解意思是"拒绝中国的茶叶"，而拒绝中国茶叶在当时就相当于拒绝了很多财富，因此"not for all the tea in China"这一习语也就延伸出"给再多的好处或金钱也不会去做"的意思。

Dutch courage

匹夫之勇；喝酒壮胆；酒后之勇

学以致用

For those who have Dutch courage, if something happens, they must first run away.

那些平日爱逞匹夫之勇的人，一旦有事，必先落荒而逃。

Joe made a hasty retreat to the local alehouse in an attempt to gain Dutch courage prior to breaking the news to Linda.

乔在把这个消息告诉琳达之前，匆忙回到当地的酒馆，喝了两杯壮胆。

We all know drink gives us all Dutch courage, and some people only dare to face difficulties after drinking wine.

众所周知，酒壮怂人胆，有些人只有喝了酒才敢直面困难。

习语故事

"Dutch courage" 是关于荷兰的习语，其字面意思是"荷兰人的勇气"。这一习语可以追溯到海洋时代，当时荷兰人和英国人在海上争夺

霸权，双方闹得不可开交，于是英国人创造了一些习语来讽刺荷兰人，"Dutch courage"就是其中之一。英国人认为荷兰人喝了酒之后就会逞匹夫之勇，于是讽刺他们"酒壮怂人胆"。由此，"Dutch courage"也就引申出了"匹夫之勇，酒后之勇"的意思。

fiddle while Rome burns
漠不关心

学以致用

Even if firms have caught up in the debt crisis, certain impervious supervisors remain fiddling while Rome burns.

就算公司已经陷入了债务危机，但某些不作为的主管们依然对此漠不关心。

We can't keep fiddling while Rome burns, and we need to pay attention to the environmental issues because global warming has affected our daily lives.

我们不能袖手旁观，我们需要重视环保问题，因为全球变暖已经影响到了我们的日常生活。

She frowned and told me that everyone else could go ahead and fiddle while Rome burns, but we had to take action to solve this problem.

她皱着眉头跟我说，别人都可以无动于衷，但是我们必须采取行动解决这个难题。

文化解读：趣说英语习语

习语故事

"fiddle while Rome burns"是与古罗马有关的习语，这一习语源自历史上著名的"罗马大火"事件。古罗马的皇帝尼禄残酷暴虐，穷奢极欲，不理朝政。公元64年，罗马城内发生了一场大火。传说，这场大火是因为尼禄不满罗马城的建筑设计，想要进行"重建"，便直接一把大火烧了整个罗马城。大火整整烧了6天，百姓流离失所，数以万计的民众因此丧生。但此时的尼禄居然坐在高塔上，弹琴作乐，兴致高昂，对百姓的遭遇漠不关心。后来，人们便用"fiddle while Rome burns"这一习语表示"漠不关心，袖手旁观"。

a New York minute
即刻，立刻

学以致用

When he saw Bob and Mark fighting on the playground, he took them to the principal's office in a New York minute.

当看到鲍勃和马克在操场上打架，他立刻把他们带到了校长的办公室。

If you come up with that price, I think customers will turn around and walk away in a New York minute.

如果你提出这个价格，我想顾客会立刻扭头就走。

I'm sorry for what I did to her and I would do it in a New York minute if there was something I could do to compensate her.

我对我对她所做的事情很抱歉，如果我可以做些事情来补偿她，我会马上去做。

习语故事

"a New York minute"是与纽约有关的习语，这一习语源于1967年左右，美国得克萨斯州人认为纽约人的生活节奏急促忙乱，一个得克萨斯州人需要很长时间才能完成的事情，一般一个纽约人可能一分钟就能做好。所以，"a New York minute"常用来表示"一瞬间，非常短暂的时间"。

文化解读：趣说英语习语

castles in Spain
白日做梦

学以致用

She keeps talking about her big-time ambitions, but it's all castles in Spain.
她一直在滔滔不绝地讲她那远大的抱负，但这都是白日做梦。

Don't build castles in Spain, and just find some work to earn money.
别再白日做梦了，找个工作挣点钱吧。

You just keep making castles in Spain all day long. Show me some results.
你整天都在白日做梦，给我看看你的成果。

习语故事

"castles in Spain"是与西班牙相关的习语，其字面意思是"西班牙城堡"。这一习语产生于 16 世纪前后，那时是西班牙航海事业的鼎盛时期。当时在西班牙国王的支持下，哥伦布出航完成了世界航行，首次发现了美洲大陆。西班牙国王还夸口建立了世界上最强大的海军。但是在 1588 年，英国人一举打败了西班牙海军，从此英国人开始嘲笑

西班牙人连自己的城堡都保护不了，还妄想称霸世界，简直是"白日做梦"。因此，"castles in Spain"这一习语后来也就有了"白日做梦"的意思，也可以指"空中楼阁，不切实际"。

习语知识

与地名相关的习语还有很多，让我们一起来看一下吧。

go Dutch　各付各的；AA制

这一习语与荷兰相关，据说几世纪前，荷兰商人与客户吃饭的时候，从来不请客，都是各自付各自的。后来"go Dutch"也就被延伸为"各付各的"的意思。这里的"go"并不是"去"的意思，而是系动词"be"，也就是"变得，变成"的意思。

it's all Greek to me　一窍不通；全然不知

这一习语与希腊相关，其最早出现于莎士比亚的历史剧《恺撒大帝》中。剧中，古罗马著名的演说家西塞罗在进行演讲，有一个叫卡斯卡的人在听，但是他一句也听不懂，因为西塞罗所讲的是希腊语。当时古罗马的官方语言虽然是拉丁语，但是希腊语是被广泛用于书籍中的语言，被誉为"高级的语言"，普通人能够接触到希腊语的机会并不多，因此卡斯卡根本听不懂。后来，"it's all Greek to me"被延伸为"一窍不通，全然不知"。

take French leave　不辞而别

"take French leave"是与法国相关的习语，众所周知，法国人爱好浪漫，他们的生活往往也会自由潇洒一些。据说十七八世纪时，法国人习惯于在参加宴会时，不告知主人就随意离开。因此，后来"take French leave"这一习语也就有了"不辞而别"的意思。

知识活学活用

学习了这么多有关颜色和地名的习语，让我们来运用一下吧。

1. 将下列句子译成中文。

（1）At the Oktoberfest, everyone is painting the town red with a big glass in hand.

（2）My mother always told me that no grades are on a silver platter, and you have to work hard.

（3）Walter's wife had just fallen ill, and when I went to see her, she went white as a sheet and felt exhausted.

（4）I was too nervous to write to you for a while. Then, having summoned Dutch courage I dared to write a letter to you.

（5）Concentrating on the minutiae of a single procedural issue, rather than on making goal planning or trying to implement the plan, is merely fiddling while Rome burns.

（6）He now appears to be training athletes with an unreasonable plan, trying to build a champion in a New York minute.

（7）Mary and I usually went Dutch when we eat, but today she suddenly asked me to eat.

（8）We were all worried that you took French leave from the party last time.

2. 将下列句子译成英文。

（1）她告诉我，我应该去伦敦找她玩，等我到了那里，我们就可以一起去狂欢痛饮。

（2）詹娜今天把自己打扮得特别漂亮，朋友都夸赞她，她感觉很开心。

（3）她有时会被误会，或许这跟她总是嬉皮笑脸有关，但她真的是一个心地善良的人。

（4）他出身名门望族，从小接受良好的教育，立志要做一名优秀的医生。

（5）如果河水漫过河岸，花园就会被淹没，但这种情况极其少见。

（6）如果这意味着我要离开我的家人，那我不会去海外工作。

（7）只有熟练地掌握技术，才能事半功倍地完成任务，否则无异于空中楼阁。

参考译文

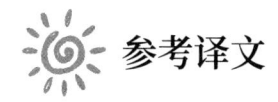

1. 译文如下。

（1）在啤酒节上，每个人手里都拿着大酒杯，开怀畅饮。

（2）妈妈一直对我说，任何成绩都不是唾手可得的，必须要付出艰苦的努力。

（3）沃特的妻子刚刚生病了，我去看望她时，她的面色苍白，感觉十分疲惫。

（4）我有段时间太紧张了，没有勇气给你写信，后来我壮着胆子给你写了一封信。

（5）只关注于程序上的细节问题，却不去制订目标规划，也不去努力实施计划，事实上这是对问题的不上心。

（6）现在，他似乎是想用一个不合理的计划培养运动员，想要立刻创造出一个冠军来。

（7）我和玛丽平时吃饭的时候都是各付各的，但是今天她突然要请我吃饭。

（8）你上次在派对上不辞而别，我们都很担心你啊。

2. 译文如下。

（1）She told me I should go to London to play with her, and when I got there we could paint the town red.

（2）Jenna dressed herself up very beautifully today, and her friends all praised her. She was tickled pink.

（3）Maybe it has something to do with her always laughing. Whilst sometimes misunderstood, she has a heart of gold.

(4) He came from a family of blue blood, received a good education since childhood, and determined to be an excellent doctor.

(5) If the river overflows its banks, the garden gets flooded; but that only happens once in a blue moon.

(6) I wouldn't work overseas for all the tea in China if it meant being away from my family.

(7) Only by proficiently mastering the technology can the task be completed with half the effort, otherwise, it is tantamount to castles in Spain.

第七章 CHAPTER 7

趣说与身体、职业相关的习语

英语习语中有很大一部分来自身体部位和职业。人们熟知身体各部位在生活中的功能，会将身体部位与周围发生的现象进行联系，从而创造了与身体相关的习语来生动地表达自己的想法。社会上的各行各业也有着自己的术语，而这些术语随着人们交往的增加，也渐渐变成了习语。这些习语生动鲜明，与生活息息相关，能让人从中领略西方文化中特有的色彩。

文化背景解读

与身体部位和职业相关的习语往往贴近生活，也能很好地表达人们的心理活动，在日常生活中运用得极为广泛。

身体与习语的关系

人体的每个部位几乎都有相对应的习语，有些习语能很好地反映人的心理情绪。例如"a sight for sore eyes"就是与眼睛有关的习语，人的视觉源自眼睛，人所看到的很多人或事情都可以通过眼睛来表达。

再比如，人们对自己的手掌都十分了解，因此当要表达对某件事十分了解时，就会说"know something like the palm of one's hand"。人们将自己熟知的身体部位与日常生活和语言交际相互联系，能够生动精确地表达自己复杂的想法。

职业对习语的影响

人们的日常生活离不开劳动，很多形象生动的习语都是来自日常的劳动，人们在劳动的过程中所创造和使用的词语，也慢慢使用到社会交际中。虽然随着社会的发展，有些职业已经渐渐淡出人们的视线，但与这些行业有关的习语一直沿用至今。

各个行业拥有不同的职业性质，因此所创造出来的习语也有不同的特色。例如"sail against the wind"就是与航海相关的习语，这一习语指的是逆风航行，表达了水手们即使身处波涛汹涌的大海上也能不畏艰难地继续航行。航海过程中诞生了很多这样的习语，这类习语大都体现了水手们的勇敢，后来也渐渐应用到了日常生活中，来赞扬某个人的勇敢坚毅。

趣说身体与习语

有关身体部位的习语往往生动形象,在日常表达中多使用这样的习语可以使英文表达更加地道。下面就来了解一些与身体部位相关的习语知识和故事吧。

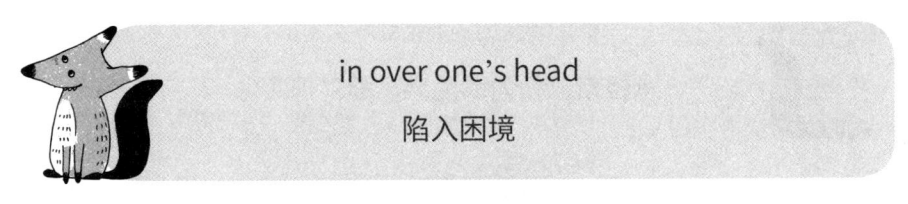

in over one's head
陷入困境

学以致用

He realized that he was in over his head, and that only his family could help him.

他意识到自己身陷困境，只有家人能帮助他。

You continue to prepare for today's report. I'll help you out if you get in over your head.

你继续准备今天的报告吧，如果你遇到困难了，我可以帮你。

We're likely getting in over our heads in this debate.

在这场辩论中，我们很可能会遇到难题。

习语故事

"in over one's head"是与头相关的习语，字面意思是"高于头顶"。这一习语最初指的是那些本来不会游泳的人，却还要在深水区游泳，深水区的水位已经没过他们的头顶，这会导致他们陷入困境。因此，"in over one's head"常用来指某人所做的事情超出了其能力范围，导致其陷入困境中。

face the music
承担自己行为的后果；面对现实

学以致用

Mary broke a window and had to face the music when her father got home.

玛丽打破了玻璃，她父亲回来以后，她肯定要承担后果。

John acknowledged what he did was wrong, had not sought to distance himself and was facing the music.
约翰承认自己的所作所为是错误的，他没有试图开脱自己，而是承担了后果。

We gently persuaded them to face the music.
我们劝说他们对自己的行为承担责任。

习语故事

"face the music"这一习语与戏剧表演中人的状态有关，当演员在舞台上表演时，一般是面对着乐池的。有时演员上了舞台后，可能会出现各种状况，如紧张、忘词等，但是无论如何，只要音乐一响，演员就没有选择的余地，只能"face the music"，继续表演下去。因此，人们便用"face the music"来表达承担后果，或者是表示面对现实，接受所有结果。

get something off one's chest
吐露心声；一吐为快；说出心里话

学以致用

I had a conversation with my friend last month, and I got things off my chest.
我上个月跟朋友谈话，吐露了我的心事。

We had a team meeting, at which we got things off our chest.
我们举行了一次团体会议，在会上我们都说出了我们的真实想法。

I like chatting with my friends on the internet, because I can get something off my chest.
我喜欢在网上和朋友聊天，因为我能把我的心事一吐为快。

习语故事

"get something off one's chest"这一习语与胸部（chest）有关，胸部在英语中往往指代的是心理活动，这可能是由于心脏正位于胸部，而心脏又象征着复杂的情绪。"get...off..."是"拿开，拿走"的意思，"get something off one's chest"的字面意思是"将一些事情从胸部拿走"，也就是"吐露心事，说出心里话"的意思。

cost an arm and a leg
价格昂贵

学以致用

Something costs an arm and a leg, but it doesn't mean it's the best thing in the world.

尽管某些东西价格昂贵，但这并不意味着它们是世界上最好的东西。

We must catch the last bus, or it will cost an arm and a leg to take a taxi from here.

我们一定要赶上最后一班公交车，不然从这里打车非常贵。

Skiing is more suitable for cold areas in the north. Practicing skiing in tropical areas will cost an arm and a leg.

滑雪这个项目更适合北方寒冷的地区，在热带地区练习滑雪成本高昂。

习语故事

"an arm and a leg"最早出现于第二次世界大战后的美国，很多士兵因为战争而失去了手臂或腿，很多报纸便称这些士兵为了保卫世界和平而付出了很大的代价。后来，"an arm and a leg"也就用来形容成本很高、代价很大的东西。

by the skin of one's teeth
侥幸成功；勉强做成

学以致用

He has escaped from going to prison by the skin of his teeth.
他侥幸逃过了牢狱之灾。

Well, I think they got out of this by the skin of their teeth.
好吧，我觉得他们只是勉强摆脱了困境。

As the ball was kicked out referee blew the full time whistle with they holding out by the skin of their teeth.
当球被踢出时，裁判吹响了全场哨声，他们侥幸赢得了这场比赛。

习语故事

"by the skin of one's teeth"这一习语是出自《圣经》中的《约伯记》，犹太人约伯在受到百般刁难后，说道："My bone cleaveth to my skin and to my flesh, and I am escaped with the skin of my teeth"，字面意思就是说"我的骨头紧贴着我的皮，紧贴着我的肉，我就用牙齿的皮肤逃脱了"。但是牙齿是没有皮肤的，其实指的是牙齿外面薄薄的一层牙釉质，这只是一个生动的比喻而已，实际意思是指"我逃出来的过程十分艰难，

只是侥幸逃脱而已"。所以，后来人们便用"by the skin of one's teeth"这一习语表示"侥幸成功，勉强做成"。

stick one's neck out
冒险行事

学以致用

We can wait until tomorrow to return this car. I'd rather pay a late fee than stick my neck out driving in this snow.

我们可以明天再去还车，我宁肯缴纳滞留金也不能冒险在雪地里开车。

You stuck your neck out when others kept their heads down and their mouths shut.

当别人都在低头闭嘴不说话的时候，你却冒险出来讲话。

Unfortunately he was sticking his neck out without realizing how serious the consequences were.

不幸的是，他在没有意识到后果有多严重的情况下，就冒险行事了。

习语故事

"stick one's neck out"是一个与颈部有关的习语，"stick"作为动

词的时候，意思比较多，但与"out"搭配，一般指的是"伸出去"的意思。"stick one's neck out"这一习语的字面意思就是"伸出了自己的脖子"。该习语原本指的是杀鸡的时候，会先斩鸡头，如果鸡把脖子伸出来就意味着有危险，因此"伸出了自己的脖子"就是在冒险行事。

vote with one's feet
避而远之；表示不满意

学以致用

As our pay falls, staff are voting with their feet and going to work elsewhere.

薪水下降导致员工们都十分不满，纷纷去了别的地方工作。

People are voting with their feet to avoid this person.

人们都对这个人避而远之。

After he said those rude things, we all voted with our feet and just walked away, leaving him standing there alone.

在他说了那些不礼貌的话之后，我们都对他避而远之，留他一个人站在那儿。

习语故事

"vote with one's feet"是一个关于脚的习语，字面意思是"用脚投票"。其原本的意思是指，人们对某件事情十分不满意，甚至选择"用脚去投票"，来表示自己的不满。这是一种夸张的表达，就是表示不赞成某件事情或是不喜欢某个东西。

习语知识

还有一部分与身体有关的习语可以根据其字面意思推断出其衍生含义，即通过生动形象的描述，可以很直观地感受到这类习语想要表达的意思。

you scratch my back and I'll scratch yours　礼尚往来

这是有关背部的习语，其中的"scratch"的意思是"挠"，整个习语的字面意思就是"你挠了我的背，我也会挠你的背"，也就是"你帮助了我，我也帮助你"的意思。汉语中的"礼尚往来"就可以很好地概括这一习语的含义。

drag one's feet　消极怠工

这是有关脚的习语，"drag one's feet"中的"drag"是"拖拽"的意思，"drag one's feet"的字面意思就是"拖拽某人的脚"，也就是不情愿去做某些事，就仿佛有人拖拽住脚一样，也就是现在常说的"拖延症"。

jump in with both feet　全心全意

这是有关脚的习语，"jump in with both feet"的字面意思很好理解，就是"两只脚都跳进去了"。两只脚都跳进去了，就是指全身心地投入进某件事情了，因此"jump in with both feet"的衍生意思就是"全心全意"。

keep someone at arm's length　敬而远之

这是关于胳膊的习语，"keep someone at arm's length"从字面上不难理解，指的是"与某人保持一臂距离"，其衍生含义也就是与某人保持距离，不与某人亲近，对某人敬而远之。

趣说职业与习语

很多习语都是人们在日常劳动的过程中创造出来的,这些与职业相关的习语在日常生活中的使用十分普遍,下面就让我们一起来学习吧。

back to the drawing board
重新开始;从头再来

学以致用

Sometimes the best way to proceed after a mistake is to go back to the drawing board.

有时候，犯了错误后继续的最好的方式就是从头再来。

After they rejected the first ideas, designers went back to the drawing board.
在他们拒绝了第一套方案后，设计师们又从头开始设计。

Perhaps it is time to go back to the drawing board and ask whether the idea of splitting the staff into three team's was the right way to go?
也许是时候重新考虑一下，把员工分为三个团队的想法是否正确？

习语故事

"back to the drawing board"是有关于设计工作的习语，"the drawing board"指的是设计师手中的"制图板"，该习语的字面意思就是"回到制图板上"，设计的第一步就是要在制图板上画出事物的雏形，而"回到制图板上"也就是指回到设计之初。由此，"back to the drawing board"也就有了"重新开始，从头再来"的意思。

rock the boat
兴风作浪；破坏现状；捣乱

学以致用

They are upset that someone is now rocking the boat and might endanger their hopes to become enriched.

现在有人在兴风作浪，可能会危及他们致富的希望，这让他们感到不安。

I really don't want to rock the boat at an important meeting, but I just feel we need to discuss Bob's recent behavior.

我并不是想在这么重要的会议上捣乱，我只是觉得我们有必要讨论一下鲍勃最近的行为。

This market can operate well so long as no one rocks the boat.

只要没人来捣乱，这个市场就能运营得很好。

习语故事

"rock the boat"是与航海有关的习语，"rock"作为动词是"摇晃"的意思，整个习语的意思就是指"摇晃船只"。我们都知道，在航行过程中，如果有人晃动船只，那么船只就会左右摇摆。如果晃动得厉害，甚至都能将船上的人翻入海里，所以在航行时是不会有人去晃动船只的，除非想要捣乱。因此，"rock the boat"就有了"捣乱"的意思。后来，"rock the boat"也衍生出"兴风作浪，破坏现状"的意思。

文化解读：趣说英语习语

in the driver's seat
掌控

学以致用

He has the ability to be in the driver's seat by taking a proactive role in coordinating team activities.

他能够掌控局面，所以在协调团队活动中发挥着积极作用。

There was no doubt that they remained firmly in the driver's seat.

毫无疑问，他们依然掌控着局面。

If the plan is to work, it will require dedication, from whoever is in the driver's seat.

如果想让这个计划成功，无论是谁掌控局面，都需要全身心投入。

习语故事

"in the driver's seat"是与司机这一职业有关的习语，字面意思是"在司机的位置"，也就是指在开车的时候坐在驾驶座。众所周知，开车的过程中，坐在驾驶座上的人掌控着方向盘，掌控着整个车辆。所以，"in the driver's seat"也就有了"掌控"的意思。

beat around the bush
兜圈子；绕圈子；旁敲侧击

学以致用

Then everybody must stop beating around the bush and tell it like it is.

大家说话不要绕圈子，应该直言不讳。

I'm busy right now, so if you have something important to tell me, stop beating around the bush and spit it out!

我现在很忙，所以如果你有重要的事情要告诉我，那就别拐弯抹角了，赶紧说出来吧！

No more beating around the bush, you tell me the truth quickly.

别再拐弯抹角了，你快告诉我真相吧。

习语故事

"beat around the bush"是与狩猎相关的习语，狩猎是一种较为古老的职业，最初的含义是"在灌木丛周围敲打"。以前的猎人为了把野兽引出来，会故意敲打灌木丛，以一种"旁敲侧击"的方法来实现狩猎的目的。后来,"beat around the bush"也衍生出"说话兜圈子、绕圈子"的意思。

take the bull by the horns
不畏艰险;勇敢地面对困难;毫不犹豫

学以致用

I've always wanted to go rock climbing and I took the bull by the horns and did it.
我一直想要去攀岩,后来我鼓起勇气去做了。

The previous auditor made a mess of paperwork, but Mary took the bull by the horns and got to work sorting it out.
尽管上一任审计员把文书工作搞得一团糟,但是玛丽还是毫不犹豫地

开始整理。

When facing difficulties, I thought we should take the initiative and take the bull by the horns.
遇到困难的时候，我认为我们应该主动出击，勇敢面对。

习语故事

"take the bull by the horns"是与斗牛有关的习语，其中的"horn"指的是公牛的角。"take the bull by the horns"的原义是指"抓住公牛的角"，当遇到公牛的袭击时，勇敢的斗牛士会面向公牛跑去，然后抓住牛的双角，以此来与公牛对峙。后来，"take the bull by the horns"便被用来形容"勇敢地面对困难，临危不惧"。

keep one's nose to the grindstone
埋头苦干

学以致用

He has kept his nose to the grindstone and has achieved great success.
他一直埋头苦干，并且取得了很好的成绩。

I must keep my nose to the grindstone and remain undisturbed by external circumstances.

我必须埋头苦干，不受外部环境的干扰。

It's about time you took a holiday, and you really have been keeping your nose to the grindstone lately.

你该去度假了，最近你真的一直在埋头苦干。

习语故事

"keep one's nose to the grindstone"是与磨刀匠相关的习语，其中的"grindstone"是磨刀器的意思。磨刀匠们在磨刀的时候，会把鼻子凑近磨刀器旁闻闻是否有烧焦味。这时候，磨刀匠的脸会贴近磨刀器，埋头苦干的样子，看起来十分努力。因此，"keep one's nose to the grindstone"就有了"努力工作，埋头苦干"的意思。

习语知识

除了上述习语，与职业相关的习语还有很多，让我们一起来学习一下吧。

show someone the ropes　传授经验

这是有关航海的习语，在航海过程中，每个水手都要学习如何系绳子，有经验的水手会向新水手传授系船绳的经验，所以"show

someone the ropes"也就衍生出"传授经验，给某人传授门道"的意思。

corner the market　垄断市场

这是与商业相关的习语，"corner the market"中的"corner"是"包围"的意思，整个习语的字面意思是"包围市场"。这是市场中的一种现象，是由一个公司生产出的商品在市场上占据了垄断地位造成的。因此，"corner the market"指的就是"垄断市场"。

知识活学活用

在学习了这么多有关身体和职业的习语之后,下面来具体运用一下吧。

1. 将下列句子译成中文。

(1) What should you do when you are in over your head in a work-related situation?

(2) I've made the biggest mistake of my life for the last years and I think it's time I finally got it off my chest.

(3) It was costing an arm and a leg and it would not have been economically acceptable to the two companies.

(4) He was full of enthusiasm, always sticking his neck out for others, and I think everyone likes him.

（5）He said teachers were voting with their feet as teaching pressure has also increased due to larger and larger class size.

（6）A loud bell rang and the children stopped their play and slowly, dragging their feet, trudging back inside.

（7）We're jumping in with both feet but at the same time being somewhat cautious, because we've both been hurt many times in the past.

（8）Determined to become a doctor from a very early age, she kept her nose to the grindstone all through high school and college.

2. 将下列句子译成英文。

（1）除非你进入前 50 名，否则你必须面对现实，而现实就是你可能没有资格参加比赛。

（2）这句话表达了两家公司之间的真正关系：互相帮助。

（3）然后，优秀的学者会从头开始，尝试调整他们最初的想法，或者提出一个新的想法。

（4）如果你明白你要为自己的生活负责，那么你就能掌控生活。

（5）如果你遇到困难了，你可以直接地告诉你的朋友们，没有必要拐弯抹角。

（6）我不知道该怎么做，我需要有经验的人给我指点迷津。

参考译文

1. 译文如下。

（1）当你对工作感到力不从心时，你应该怎么做？

（2）在过去的几年中，我犯了我一生中最大的错误，我想是时候吐露出来了。

（3）这个项目耗资巨大，这两家公司在经济上无法接受。

（4）他热情似火，总是勇于冒险，我认为大家都喜欢他。

（5）他说，由于班级规模越来越大，导致教学压力也随之增加，因此教师们都十分不满。

（6）上课铃声响起，孩子们停下游戏，慢慢吞吞地艰难地回到教室里。

（7）我们全心全意地投入，但同时保持谨慎，因为我们过去都曾经受过很多次伤害。

（8）她从小就决心要成为一名医生，在高中和大学期间她一直努力学习。

2. 译文如下。

（1）Unless you are in the top 50, you have to face the music, and the music is that you may not be eligible for the competition.

（2）This statement expresses the real relations between the two companies: you scratch my back and I'll scratch yours.

（3）The good scholars then go back to the drawing board and try to tweak their original idea, or come up with a new one.

（4）If you understand that you are responsible for your own life, you are in the driver's seat.

（5）If you get stuck, you can tell your friends directly. There is no need to beat around the bush.

（6）I don't have a clue about how to do this, and I need someone with experience to show me the ropes.

CHAPTER 8

第八章

读懂与体育、娱乐运动有关的习语

随着各类运动盛会的举办，越来越多的体育和娱乐运动走入人们的生活。体育本身就是先民娱乐的一种形式，早在古埃及的时候，就已经有击剑、射箭等一系列运动项目了。在体育、娱乐运动发展过程中，也造就了许多有趣的习语，这类习语一直沿用至今。这些习语所包含的民族特色不言而喻，正确掌握它们的用法，能够更好地理解和使用英语。

文化背景解读

在西方体育和娱乐运动发展的过程中，形成了很多与之相关的习语。这些习语作为西方文化的一部分，反映了体育与娱乐运动对文化的影响。

体育运动对习语的影响

体育运动是西方文化中的重要组成部分，其所凝聚的竞争精神对文化的影响十分显著，对人类社会的发展更是贡献了一份力量。世界

上最具代表性的体育赛事便是奥林匹克运动会，奥运会起源于古希腊。地中海沿岸的古希腊是一个拥有数百个岛屿的岛国，其地域环境恶劣，土地贫瘠，在这样的地理环境下，古希腊人奋起抗争，创造了多种体育项目来激励当地人民，这造就了古希腊人的冒险性格和抗争意识。

　　倡导竞争、拼搏、自由的体育运动和体育精神，一直不断延续，不仅影响着社会生活，也影响着人们的语言，并由此产生了很多习语。这些习语大部分都是与体育规则相关的，反映着体育精神，体现了体育对文化的影响。

娱乐运动对习语的影响

　　自14世纪欧洲文艺复兴运动兴起，各种娱乐活动渐渐走入人们的生活中。在古老的欧洲社会，等级制度森严，上流社会的生活往往充

斥着各种休闲娱乐活动，他们也将这些娱乐活动作为贵族身份的象征。因此，西方文化中的娱乐活动大都有着典雅、高贵的特征。

例如，赛马、音乐会、戏剧表演、魔术表演等休闲活动已经成为人们文化生活的重要内容，也已经成为人们进行文化和感情交流的一种方式，甚至成为一种社交需要，逐渐形成了大量与之相关的习语。其中，与赛马、棋牌游戏相关的习语比比皆是，而且用途甚广。尤其是赛马，是英美国家十分重要的一项娱乐活动，著名的习语"dark horse"（黑马）就源于赛马活动，后来被人们广泛应用于生活之中。

趣说体育运动与习语

与体育运动有关的习语，源自篮球、板球、棒球等项目的居多，下面就来了解一些与体育运动相关的习语知识和故事吧。

full-court press
全面出击

学以致用

From now on we will be in a full-court press to prevent this dispute from happening.

从现在开始我们要尽一切努力阻止这场纠纷的发生。

The supporters of the bill launched a full-court press to help it pass.

这项法案的支持者发起了全面攻势来帮助它通过。

The company planned a full-court press to beat its competitors during the Spring Festival.

这家公司计划在春节期间全面出击来打败其他竞争对手。

He can only get through this difficult time if we use a full-court press to help him.

只有我们全力以赴地去帮助他，他才能渡过这个难关。

习语故事

"full-court press"在篮球运动中指的是"全场紧逼"战术，其中"full-court"指的是整个球场，而"press"指的就是施压。"全场紧逼"战术是指在由攻转守的时候，在全场范围内紧紧盯住对手，通过个人防守和团队配合，达到转守为攻的一种防御战术。这种战术破坏力极强，效果也绝佳。"full-court press"也多被应用到生活中，表示"全面出击"，一般也可以指尽全力做某事或全力以赴做某事。

文化解读：趣说英语习语

on a sticky wicket
处于不利地位

学以致用

The engagement with him made us on a sticky wicket.
与他的交战使我们陷入不利境地。

If so, many merchants are on a sticky wicket and must carefully adjust their business models.
这样的话，许多商家就会处于不利地位，必须小心调整自己的业务模式。

In this debate, she was on a sticky wicket due to her inexperience.
在这场辩论中，她缺乏经验，导致自己处于不利地位。

习语故事

板球兴起于英国，被誉为贵族运动，也是英国的国球。在板球运动中，有一项规则便是将球击入三柱门，而"wicket"指的就是三柱门。板球运动对场地要求很高，如果这个场地十分泥泞（sticky），就会导致无法将球击中。因此，"on a sticky wicket"就有了"处于不利地位"的意思。

touch all the bases
面面俱到

学以致用

We has managed to touch all the bases necessary, and trade goes on.
我们想方设法把所有的事情都处理妥当，生意也维持了下来。

He touched all the bases to explain everything, and all related issues were properly resolved.
他的说明面面俱到，凡是相关的问题都进行了妥善解决。

Not only are my friends very capable, but also they touch all the bases in everything they do.
我的朋友不但能力很强，做起事情来更是面面俱到。

习语故事

棒球是美国的国球，这种运动为英语创造了不少习语，其中"touch all the bases"就是十分典型的一个。"touch all the bases"在棒球中指的是遍触全垒的意思，在棒球运动中，共有四个垒位，分别是一垒、二垒、三垒以及本垒。这四个垒位共同构成一个菱形的区域，棒

文化解读：趣说英语习语

球运动员击球后，必须触遍这四个垒位才能得分。因此，现在人们常常用"touch all the bases"来表示做事情面面俱到，可以全面照顾到每一处。

step up to the plate
开始行动

学以致用

We need to step up to the plate to care for children who are starving.
我们需要行动起来去关心那些挨饿的孩子们。

In any case, developers must step up to the plate to solve this problem.
无论如何，开发商必须出面解决这个问题。

We must step up to the plate immediately and develop feasible solutions to help those affected by the earthquake.
我们必须马上采取措施制订可行的方案来帮助那些地震中的灾民。

We nominated Johnson to step up to the plate to negotiate with Mrs Smith.
我们提名了约翰逊出面与史密斯夫人谈判。

习语故事

在棒球运动中，内野是由本垒、一垒、二垒、三垒围绕的菱形，菱形下方的那个角就是棒球赛的中心，也就是本垒。棒球运动中，"plate"指的是本垒板。当一名棒球运动员踏上本垒板的时候，就意味着这名棒球运动员要开始击球了。因此，人们现在常会用"step up to the plate"表示开始做某事，或表示由某人出面解决问题。

straight from the shoulder
直截了当地

学以致用

Please tell me straight from the shoulder.
请直言不讳地告诉我吧。

This was a criticism straight from the shoulder and there was no way to conceal my embarrassment.

这是公开的批评,我无法掩饰自己的尴尬。

In the end I had to speak straight from the shoulder.

最后我不得不直截了当地说了。

习语故事

"straight from the shoulder"这一习语源自拳击运动,早在百年前就开始使用了,其中"shoulder"指的是肩膀,"straight from the shoulder"的字面意思就是直接攻击肩膀部位,这种攻击既狠又重,出拳时几乎用上了全身力气。因此,"straight from the shoulder"就有了"直截了当"的意思,现在常用于表示说话直言不讳,而且说话的时候不顾及对方感情是否会受到伤害。

below the belt
暗箭伤人;不公正的

学以致用

He stressed: "This insult was a way below the belt, untrue and unjust."

他强调说:"这种侮辱简直是暗箭伤人,是不正确的也是不公正的。"

There was a very derogatory comment made about a particular person and it was below the belt, and should never have gone out.
这些对某人的贬损性言论是不公正的，不应该发表出去。

Don't you think you will be striking below the belt if you ask someone else to compete for you?
你让别人替你参加比赛，你不觉得这样是违反规则的吗？

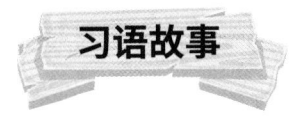

习语故事

1867年，一名名叫钱伯斯的拳击手为拳击比赛制定了一套规则，其中最引人注目的就是在比赛中不允许攻击对手腰带以下的身体部位，否则就按照犯规处理。这项规则是为了保护比赛双方的安全，也为了彰显体育的公平公正。后来，人们就将"below the belt"比喻不公正的行为或事情。"below the belt"也常与"hit"连用，表示暗箭伤人。

习语知识

与体育相关的习语还有很多，下面的一些也十分经典，我们一起来了解一下吧。

not get to the first base　出师不利

这是源于棒球比赛的习语，如果运动员未能赶在垒球到第一垒的

时候跑到第一垒，就表示比赛时"出师不利"。

keep the ball rolling　说话、活动等不中断

这是源于足球比赛的习语，足球比赛中，一旦开场后，球就会一直不停地在场上滚动，如果球不动了，那比赛时的气氛也就无法延续了。同样，在很多重大场合或比赛中，要保持活动、说话不能中断。对此，人们常使用"keep the ball rolling"来表示保持气氛的延续。

play cricket　光明正大

这是源于板球比赛的习语，板球比赛规则复杂但很讲究公平公正，因此，"play cricket"常比喻光明正大，遵守比赛规则。反之，"not cricket"则比喻没有绅士风度，做事不光明磊落。

slam dunk　辉煌的胜利

这是源于篮球比赛的习语，"slam dunk"原义是大力扣篮，在篮球比赛中，扣篮绝对是篮球场上最精彩的一幕，因此后来人们常用"slam dunk"来形容辉煌的胜利。

jump the gun　抢先一步

这是源于赛跑的习语，众所周知，赛跑运动员都需要等到信号枪的指令发出后才能开跑。"gun"就是指赛场上的信号枪，但有些运动员会在信号枪响之前就起跑了，这就是抢跑。因此，"jump the gun"常用来比喻过早或仓促地抢先一步做某事。

趣说娱乐运动与习语

西方文化中，娱乐的地位举足轻重，因此便诞生了许多相关的习语，这些习语体现着西方的娱乐文化，并沿用至今。

> give somebody free rein
> 给某人充分的自由

学以致用

Marry gave me free rein of both her kitchen and her bedchamber.

玛丽允许我自由支配她的厨房和卧室。

He can not comprehend what prompts others to give their heart free rein.
他无法理解是什么促使他人放纵自己的心。

My mom gave me free rein and allowed me to do as many things as I wanted.
我的妈妈给了我很多自由，让我可以随心所欲做很多事。

习语故事

"give somebody free rein"源自赛马运动，原义是指"give the horse free rein"，即骑士松开缰绳，给予马匹自由，允许马按照自己的节奏自由行走。这一习语后来被用于形容给予某人充分的自由，支持某人做事情。

across the board
全面；整体

学以致用

The two main aims were achieved across the board.

这两个主要的目标全部实现了。

Jobs will be lost across the board, in manufacturing, marketing, and administration.
制造业、营销和行政部门的工作岗位将全面流失。

The changes, if reported correctly, will cause problems right across the board.
如果报告正确,这些改变将导致问题全面爆发。

习语故事

"across the board"是赛马中一个常见的术语,表示下注时选择全线下注,就是把赌注下在有望取得前三名的马或其中任何一匹上,这是一种综合性赌注。这样无论马跑第一、第二还是第三都无所谓,投注人都可以赢钱。

dead heat
势均力敌;不分胜负

学以致用

Last year the Florida race was, in effect, a dead heat.

去年佛罗里达州的比赛实际上是平局。

If you look merely at voting margins, there is a dead heat.
如果你只看投票率,结果不分胜负。

We play for about 40 minutes to a dead heat at game point.
我们在赛点上打了40分钟,最后是平局。

习语故事

"dead heat"源于赛马,是一个技术术语。在赛马比赛中,"heat"指的是个人预赛,然而在多数比赛中,平局的比赛是不算数的。"dead"除了表示"死的",还可以表示"被废弃的,不作数的",因此所有以平局告终的比赛最后都被称为"dead heat"。后来,"dead heat"就引申出"势均力敌"的意思。

champing at the bit
等不及做某事

学以致用

The kids are champing at the bit to go to the park. Can you take them?

孩子们等不及想去公园了，你能带他们去吗？

Now that my daughter is 16, she's champing at the bit to take the driving test.
现在我的女儿 16 岁了，她已经等不及想要去参加驾驶证考试了。

The dogs were champing at the bit to begin the hunt.
猎狗们已经争先恐后地开始狩猎。

习语故事

"champing at the bit"源自赛马。"bit"指的是一根金属棒，通常是放在马嘴里连接到缰绳上的。一些骑马者会在比赛之前寻找一直在咀嚼或啃咬金属棒的马，他们认为马的这种行为是一种准备奔跑的标志。后来，"champing at the bit"就有了"准备好并且已经等不及要去做某些事"的意思。

pass the buck
推卸责任

学以致用

Shouldn't we now be acknowledging blame rather than passing the buck?
我们现在不是应该承认责任而非推卸责任吗？

Have you ever noticed that the folks who spend so much time talking about "responsibility" are usually the first to try to pass the buck?

你有没有注意到花这么多时间谈论"责任"的人通常是第一个试图推卸责任的人?

It's easy to pass the buck and blame someone else for your failure.

推卸责任并将失败归咎于他人很容易。

习语故事

"pass the buck"是产生于扑克牌桌上的习语。早年在美国西部人们经常佩戴一把猎刀,在玩扑克牌的时候,就会传递这样一把猎刀,为的是轮流坐庄发牌的时候不会混淆,谁坐庄谁就会拿着猎刀。发完牌后再把猎刀传递给下一个人。"pass the buck"也就是指把发牌的责任交给下个人了,由此"pass the buck"就引申出"推卸责任"的意思。

ace in the hole
隐藏的王牌;锦囊妙计

学以致用

His embarrassing secret is my ace in the hole, and I plan to reveal it to everyone the next time he mocks me publicly.

他令人尴尬的秘密是我的王牌，我打算下次他公开嘲笑我时向所有人透露。

He gave a slow grin and immediately told Jade that he had an ace in the hole.

他慢慢地咧嘴一笑，立刻告诉杰德他还有一张王牌。

Mary's beautiful singing voice was her ace in the hole in case everything else failed.

即使一切都失败时，玛丽美妙的歌声依然是她的王牌。

习语故事

"ace in the hole"来自纸牌游戏。最先开始发牌的时候，每个玩家的头一张牌都会扣着，谁也看不见这张底牌是什么。然后再发几张明牌给每个玩家，每次发一张，就会进行一次下注。只有最后翻牌时，才知道最终谁是赢家。"ace"是纸牌中的A，"in the hole"则是"隐藏"的意思。"ace in the hole"的意思就是隐藏起来的A，在最危急的时刻，将其拿出就可以反败为胜。因此，"ace in the hole"后来就有了"秘密武器，锦囊妙计"的意思。

bet the farm

孤注一掷；破釜沉舟

学以致用

I've got investments with two companies because I'm afraid of betting the farm with one company.

我在两家公司都进行了投资，因为我害怕在一家公司身上孤注一掷。

Don't bet the farm when you go to Las Vegas! It's better to take what you're willing to lose in cash.

去拉斯维加斯不要孤注一掷！最好只拿你想要下注的现金。

I know you won't bet the farm on it, but I know I'm going to be famous one day.

我知道你不会完全信任我，但我知道我有一天会成名。

习语故事

"bet the farm"源自棋牌游戏。在下注时，大手的玩家在下注筹码时可能会将全部的钱都押进去，这就意味着玩家想要将所有的家产都

押在这一轮比赛的结果上。"farm"指的是农场,在这里就借指全部家产。现在,"bet the farm"这一习语常用于表示"孤注一掷"。

习语知识

除了以上习语,其实还有很多习语来自娱乐运动,让我们一起来认识一下吧。

ace up one's sleeve　锦囊妙计

"ace up one's sleeve"与"ace in the hole"的意思差不多,都是隐藏王牌的意思,都比喻在关键时刻拿出来解救危机的办法。

hold one's cards close to one's vest　不让别人知道你在做什么

该习语源自棋牌游戏,是指在进行棋牌游戏的时候,将自己的牌隐藏起来。按照字面意思就是将自己的牌放入马甲中,也就是隐藏自己的牌,不让别人知道自己的牌,后来表示不让别人知道自己在做什么。

stack up against　比较;较量

该习语来自棋牌游戏,指的是将筹码牌堆积起来进行比较。后来,延伸为"比较,较量"的意思。

知识活学活用

在学习了这么多有关体育和娱乐运动的习语之后,下面来具体运用一下吧。

1. 将下列句子译成中文。

(1) I don't want to put the full-court press on him if he doesn't like me.

(2) My mail indicates that this country needs people who are willing to sit down and give straight from the shoulder advice.

(3) Maybe you are jumping the gun and are actually feeling uncomfortable about the situation yourself, not about what other people

are thinking.

（4）It allows schools to build a studying centre, and use this center to raise standards across the board.

（5）Everybody is champing at the bit to get involved and I am very confident we will raise the funds required.

（6）Instead they have been engaged in passing the buck, and shifting all blame onto the staff.

（7）He was working on something to get her out of this. Perhaps even now he had an ace up his sleeve.

（8）To be honest, I have always known that the insult was below the belt.

（9）We've heard nothing but praise for this film so far, but strangely it gets two stars across the board from the website.

2. 将下列句子译成英文。

（1）由于不断有余震袭来，救援工作陷入了困境之中。

（2）我今天要做的就是要全面实施这项措施，并继续进行良好的对话。

（3）这段描述特别有说服力，主要针对的是保险公司推卸责任和逃避责任。

（4）这家公司拥有隐藏的王牌，因为它拥有独一无二的人才和想法。

（5）现在并不是孤注一掷的好时机。

（6）我不知道他们看了多久才宣布这是平局，但时间好像没有看

起来那么长。

（7）电话推销员可以自由地往您家里打电话。

（8）我们希望人们能开始接种疫苗，只有这样才能保证健康。

参考译文

1. 译文如下。

（1）如果他不喜欢我，我不想对他步步紧逼。

（2）我的这封邮件表明这个国家需要愿意坐下来并且直接给出建议的人。

（3）或许是你自己操之过急，事实上你自己是对这种情况感到不适，而不是对别人的想法。

（4）学校因而得以建立一个学习中心，并利用这个中心全面提高标准。

（5）每个人都在争先恐后地参与进来，我非常有信心我们会筹集到所需的资金。

（6）相反，他们一直在推卸责任，并将所有责任推给员工。

（7）他正在想办法让她摆脱困境，也许即使现在他还有一张王牌。

（8）老实说，我一直都知道这种侮辱是不公平的。

（9）到目前为止，我们只听到了对这部电影的赞美，但奇怪的是，它在网上总共才获得了两颗星。

2. 译文如下。

（1）Rescue efforts have been on a sticky wicket by aftershocks.

（2）All I'm doing today is touching all the bases to implement this measure and continuing to have good dialogue.

（3）This description is particularly persuasive, focusing on the insurance company passing the buck and avoiding responsibility.

（4）This company has an ace up its sleeve, because the company abounds in talent and ideas like no other.

（5）This isn't a great time to bet the farm.

（6）I don't know how long they looked at the tape before they declared it a dead heat, but it could not have been as long as it seemed.

（7）Telemarketers are given free rein to call your home.

（8）We want people to step up to the plate to be vaccinated, and that's the only way to stay healthy.

参考文献

[1] Dean, John. 当代美国短语习语词典 [M]. 楚向群，等，编译. 北京：外文出版社，2003.

[2] 陈慧. 英语习语研究：理论与实践 [M]. 南京：南京大学出版社，2018.

[3] 候继云. 英语基础习语 [M]. 哈尔滨：黑龙江人民出版社，1986.

[4] 李雪冬，周霓忻，王瑞红. 常用英语习语翻译与应用 [M]. 天津：天津科学技术出版社，2018.

[5] 林丽霞. 英语习语文化探源及翻译研究 [M]. 北京：中央编译出版社，2021.

[6] 刘彬. 英语习语语义的认知研究 [M]. 徐州：中国矿业大学出版社，2007.

[7] 刘凯. 英汉习俗及习语的文化对比研究 [M]. 北京：中国时代经济出版社，2014.

[8] 陆阳. 习语的语用翻译研究 [M]. 徐州：中国矿业大学出版社，

2006.

[9] 骆世平.英语习语研究[M].上海：上海外语教育出版社，2006.

[10] 魏福利.学会美国习语[M].石家庄：河北科学技术出版社，2009.

[11] 徐式赞.英语习语基础[M].开封：河南教育出版社，1986.

[12] 张镇华，等.英语习语的文化内涵及其语用研究[M].北京：外语教学与研究出版社，2007.

[13] 程超轶.基于概念转喻的英汉身体部位习语对比研究[D].成都：西南交通大学，2017.

[14] 于静.英汉基本颜色习语的隐喻用法比较分析[D].西安：西安工业大学，2015.

[15] 陈媛媛.五颜六色的英语：颜色习语中英应用对比[J].语文学刊（外语教育教学），2014（8）：14-16.

[16] 段小卫.浅谈源于体育娱乐的英语习语[J].科技信息（科学教研），2007（24）：191，215.

[17] 李加强.谈与身体部位有关的英语习语[J].华东冶金学院学报（社会科学版），2000（2）：105-108.

[18] 林瑞娟.浅析英语习语、谚语、典故与西方文化[J].甘肃科技纵横，2005（6）：190，40.

[19] 刘萍.英语动植物习语探源[J].英语沙龙（实战版），2005（7）：25.

[20] 刘晓碚.浅议中西典故习语在翻译中的运用[J].嘉应大学学报，2000（4）：67-71.

[21] 刘颖.浅议地理和宗教对英汉习语的影响[J].南平师专学报，

2005（3）：119-121.

[22] 司徒平.《圣经》人物典故及相关习语浅析[J].考试周刊，2011（52）：47-48.

[23] 王瑞雪.浅谈希腊罗马神话对英语词汇的影响[J].今古文创，2020（43）：81-82.

[24] 王珍，冯学民.西方牌戏对英语习语的影响[J].疯狂英语（教师版），2007（5）：51-53，61.

[25] 夏海玲，陈午祎.与身体部位相关的英语习语的修辞意义和语义学分析[J].科教文汇（下旬刊），2015（4）：178-179.

[26] 徐歆玉.英国地理特征影响下的英语习语与跨文化交际[J].高等财经教育研究，2014（4）：48-51.

[27] 杨艳群.体育娱乐文化对英语习语的影响及其翻译[J].文史博览（理论），2012（5）：26-27，36.

[28] 张静.英语习语、典故与古希腊罗马神话[J].湖北函授大学学报，2012（8）：143-144.

[29] 朱志霖，周美兰.动植物词语在英语习语中的应用与翻译[J].阜新矿业学院学报，1985（4）：144-152.

[30] 訾韦力.英语习语中颜色词的认知解析[J].海外英语，2014（5）：265-267.